ENDORSEMENTS

Chris Gore's *Walking in Supernatural Healing* draws the reader into the adventure and joy of partnering with God in the miraculous. I have had the privilege of watching Chris' hunger firsthand. His passion for God and his heart for people bearing affliction have been amazing. Most important is that his passion was not deterred when he saw little to no results when praying for the sick. This hurdle is a vital one to cross, which he did nobly. He flew across the world to pursue activation that would bring breakthrough to see it happen through his own life. This book will be an encouragement to anyone looking to operate in a lifestyle of the supernatural. And now his amazing breakthroughs can become yours.

BILL JOHNSON
Pastor, Bethel Church, Redding CA
Author of *When Heaven Invades Earth* and *Hosting the Presence*

Chris Gore is a powerfully anointed minister of healing, a clear communicator of the truth of God's word regarding healing. He is an experienced minister of healing. Chris is not an armchair theologian, but a practitioner of healing. He writes with the exciting style of a man with lots of stories of God's power to heal. Truth and testimony are blended in an exciting, entertaining, educating way. You don't want to miss the blessings that will be yours through reading Chris' new book, Walking in Supernatural Healing Power.

RANDY CLARK
Founder and President of Global Awakening and
the Apostolic Network of Global Awakening

Chris Gore's book, *Walking in Supernatural Healing Power* needs to be on every believer's bookshelf. You may think that the healing ministry is something that belongs to those in the pulpit or is reserved exclusively for spiritual "superstars." This book will shift that way of thinking, as Chris reveals how accessible supernatural ministry is to every believer—including *you*. He goes where few others ever have, tackling the "tough questions" head on, dealing with common roadblocks to healing—offense and disappointment to name two—and finally, he makes the center of the book... *Jesus*. It is a pleasure to recommend this book, as I believe it is going to radically impact the way supernatural healing is approached and activated in the global church. Get ready to be equipped to successfully flow in God's healing power!

LARRY SPARKS
Director of Curriculum Resources, Destiny Image Publishers
Host, *Voice of Destiny* Radio Program

This book's message WILL change your life! If you allow God to speak to you as you read this, it will revolutionize how you see yourself and renew your mind in ways that will produce dramatic results in your life and the lives of those around you! I've read a lot of books over the years on healing, but none have gone to the heart of the issues like Chris does in *Walking in Supernatural Healing Power*. In a very genuine and practical way, he lays out the common roadblocks to experiencing God's healing power and demonstrates the characteristics of a life wholly obedient to God's voice and nature. Well done Chris!!

RONDA RANALLI
Director of Content Acquisitions, Destiny Image Publishers

You cannot be with Chris Gore for more than 5 minutes and not be impacted by his passion; passion for God, passion for the Kingdom of God to be manifested into today's world and passion for the body of Christ to walk in the full empowerment of all that we were called to walk in. This book is not about information—you are about to embark on a journey of empowerment, encouragement and revelation. Standing on a thoroughly biblical foundation Chris shares with us his own story, the hardships, the pain, and also the breakthroughs and the victory. His passion and love for God and the people of God shine through every page as he opens up to us a clear understanding of the supernatural power of healing and gives us very practical steps to have the confidence to step out and begin to see the power of God work through them. I am sure that this book is destined to be a classic and will become a standard read for every pastor and in every church and healing room that desires to see the glory of God manifest and an increase in the healing ministry.

TRENT HODSON
Senior Leader, Liberty Christian Church, Auckland, New Zealand

While I love the outrageous healing miracles Chris sees, his personal integrity, his refreshing honesty and humor, and that he is a family man; what I love most about Chris is that he is a friend of the Holy Spirit. Healing for him flows out of intimacy and identity. Chris teaches us **who** we are and **Whose** we are. This is a book on healing that anyone can relate to. If you don't "feel" the Holy Spirit when you pray, if you have never seen anybody healed, if you only see healing sporadically, if you are offended at God for someone not healed, or you want to go to another level, then Chris' book will equip your head and heart to move into the healing ministry of Jesus.

JIM BAKER
Senior Pastor, Zion Christian Fellowship, Powell, OH

As Director of the Bethel Church Healing Room, traveling healing minister and teacher, Chris Gore has done a wonderful work in writing this book. Whether you are just beginning your quest for knowledge and understanding about healing or are already well seasoned in healing, this book will provide revelation about the supernatural realm of God and how you can work in that realm to fulfill your destiny in God. The truth of the Word of God, mixed with the testimonies of healing that confirm the Word, will produce great faith in the reader. Chris inspires us to activate Colossians 3:2, "Set your mind on the things above, not on the things that are on earth." We are reminded that the power to heal the sick is God's power, not ours. It is the relationship with God that brings His power through us to fulfill His will on earth—to heal His people. Be inspired as you read this book.

CAL PIERCE
International Director, Healing Rooms Ministries

The book *Walking in Supernatural Healing Power* is such an encouragement and extreme help for everyone who wants to grow and reach for more in the area of healing. Chris Gore is a man with a big theoretical knowledge about healing but even more he is very much experienced through his life journey. Those challenges, fights and breakthroughs make his message very authentic and real to us.

RUEDI ALTORFER
Pastor, GvC Winterthur, Switzerland

WALKING IN
SUPERNATURAL
HEALING
POWER

⊗

CHRIS GORE

Chris Gore wishes to thank Destiny image for removing any copyright issues that pertain directly to the healing/miracle testimonies that are used in this book. They are not owned by any person or that any person would take credit but that each and every testimony is for God's glory and He delights in them. Psalm 119:111

DESTINY IMAGE® PUBLISHERS, INC.

P.O. Box 310, Shippensburg, PA 17257-0310

"Promoting Inspired Lives."

This book and all other Destiny Image, Revival Press, MercyPlace, Fresh Bread, Destiny Image Fiction, and Treasure House books are available at Christian bookstores and distributors worldwide.

For a U.S. bookstore nearest you, call 1-800-722-6774.

For more information on foreign distributors, call 717-532-3040.

Reach us on the Internet: www.destinyimage.com.

ISBN 13 TP: 978-0-7684-4242-7

ISBN 13 Ebook: 978-0-7684-8463-2

For Worldwide Distribution, Printed in the U.S.A.

6 7 8 / 17 16

DEDICATION

I dedicate this book to my amazing wife, Liz, and daughters, Charlotte, Emma, and Sophie. Liz, you have been the most amazing continual source of encouragement and inspiration. You continued to believe in me that I could write this book, even when at times I did not believe that I could, myself. I love you each so very much.

You are wildly loved.

Much Grace

Chris

ACKNOWLEDGMENTS

I want to acknowledge the many spiritual parents in my life and the input that they have had into my life over the past number of years. I want to give special thanks to Bill Johnson, Kris Vallotton, and Randy Clark for the way that they have helped to shape and renew my thinking and have helped me become the person that God always wanted me to be.

The values that they have installed into my life are the values of the Kingdom.

Authors note

Several of the testimonies that are shared in this book are so powerful that they, for the protection of the individual involved and to ensure that they walk their healing out in fullness of the heart of God, have had their names or gender changed.

I also wish to thank Destiny Image for not requiring a copyright on the testimonies that are shared. It was a big deal to me that the testimonies did not become copyrighted, as they are the in fact the testimonies of Jesus!

> *Your testimonies I have taken as a heritage forever, For they are the rejoicing of my heart.* (Psalm 119:111)

CONTENTS

INTRODUCTION

Just a few years ago I would never have imagined the journey that the Lord was about to take us on as a family. I had longed to see the supernatural flowing through me and had prayed for around 1,000 people with no result over a ten-year period. In 2005 everything changed, and today I have the joy of seeing many thousands of lives touched by the healing/miracle power of Jesus.

I so desire to see the body of Christ arise and come into their identity and destiny that together we would see Jesus get the full reward of His suffering. I desire to see the body not just having supernatural experiences but that our supernatural experiences would line up with the Word of God. I love to see people who know the Word of God and allow His word to lead them into an encounter with God Himself..

While there is no formula or magic wand to walking in supernatural power, there is a renewing of the mind that needs to take place. This book has some principles on operating in the supernatural so that we can all be released into a greater dimension of miracles and healings. But the core of the book is more to address the heart of healing, that will help thrust you into your destiny and deepen your relationship with God, so that you would begin to see such incredible fruitfulness through your life like you could once only have dreamed of. While there is often mystery in the healing ministry, the heart of this book is to demystify it as much as possible, so that the greater Church would be equipped and empowered to show that we are all destined and designed to walk in the supernatural healing power of Jesus.

You will be challenged and inspired as you read the journey of one man's walk into the supernatural healing power. You will see what God can do with any life that is surrendered to Jesus, intent on getting all that He paid for.

CHAPTER 1

---------- ℭℨ ----------

A SOLID FOUNDATION

In the late '90s I went to my senior pastor one day and declared to him that I was going to commence a lifetime fast until I saw breakthrough. I was really hoping that he would talk me out of it, but his only words of comfort were to be careful. So now that I had committed to this, I had to carry it through. The first day was easy and the second day I was getting hungry, but by the third day I really thought I was going to die. I came home from work one night and fell on the couch and called my wife and said, "I feel so hungry and so sick that I really feel like I could die." My wife gave me two options: break the fast and eat or die, but if I chose the latter option, then to do it quietly. She left the room laughing, and I had to make a decision, as I was miserable. I chose to break the fast and went to the fridge and ate an entire packet of sausages and a whole loaf of bread. I really thought I was going to die after that; I felt so much worse.

No matter how much we do in works, I have found that it is never enough. You read three chapters of the Bible and the enemy comes along and says, "If you had read six chapters, you would have gotten a break-through." You pray for 60 minutes and that same voice says, "Maybe you should have prayed for two hours and you might have had your breakthrough." You fast for 21 days, and that condemning voice of the accuser whispers in your ear, "Maybe a back-to-back, 21-day fast would have gotten you what you need."

Often we do works-oriented things out of a place of desperation to see God move or to please Him, as we believe that the things that we do will cause God to love us more, and the supernatural will flow. This mentality leaves us in a position of working *for* God's love as opposed to working *from* God's love. I spent many years working hard for His love because of the lack of revelation on just how much He already loved me and liked me. Many Christians may know that God loves them, but when you question them, they really have no revelation on just how much God also likes them. Though they know in their heads that God loves them, they may also believe the lie that God just tolerates them. God likes to hang out with us and to do the things that we like to do.

WORKING FROM LOVE

When we have the revelation of His love, grace, and goodness, then we really begin to understand that He can't love us any more than He already does. The apostles Peter and John are two of my favorite people in the Bible. It appears that they were wired totally differently.

> *Now there was leaning on Jesus' bosom one of His disciples, whom Jesus loved* (John 13:23).

The Bible calls John in this passage "the disciple whom Jesus loved," so we could take from that that Jesus loved John the most. It's interesting that this phrase only appears in the Gospel of John, of which John is the author.

So what exactly was John doing? We know without question that Jesus loved all the disciples intensely, but I believe that John had a revelation that maybe the other disciples did not have. John knew that he was loved. Could it be that John was the disciple who most knew how to practice enjoying the presence of Jesus and His love for John?

On the night of the Last Supper, Jesus made a statement that must have been hard for the disciples to take. He told them they would all fail Him and they would all fall away from Him.

I am sure they were all shocked because without question, they all loved Jesus so much. When Jesus said this, Peter took Jesus aside and essentially agreed with Jesus that the rest of the disciples would probably fail Him, but "not me," he said to Jesus.

> *Peter said to Him, "Even if all are made to stumble, yet I will not be."*
>
> *Jesus said to him, "Assuredly, I say to you that today, even this night, before the rooster crows twice, you will deny Me three times."*
>
> *But he spoke more vehemently, "If I have to die with You, I will not deny You!"*
>
> *And they all said likewise* (Mark 14:29-31).

The setting in John 13:23 was during the Last Supper. We see the disciples at the table with the Lord, including the two I have mentioned, Peter and John.

At the table we could say that there were two kinds of Christians represented. One was represented by Peter, whose name means "stone" or "rock," and if we break that down further, means "law." Peter represents the believers who declare their love for the Lord, just as we all do. John's name means "beloved," "loved one," or broken down further, means "grace." Now John leaning on the breast of Jesus is a picture of depending on the Lord's love for him; he represents every believer who declares the Lord's love for them. We could say that one represents Christians under the law, and the other represents Christians under grace.

But the one who was always declaring how much he loved Jesus, before the night was out, was found denying Him three times, while the one who was dependent on the Lord's love for him was there to minister to Jesus at the time of His greatest need.

On the night of the Last Supper, when Jesus said, "One of you will betray me," Peter turned to John and asked, "Who is it?" Even there, there was a distance between Peter and Jesus. Why did Peter not ask Jesus Himself who the betrayer would be?

Jesus knew that each of the disciples would fail Him. But Peter's dependence on his love for Jesus instead of a solid foundation of Jesus' love for him actually caused him to fail Jesus in His time of need.

Jesus said that each of them would fail Him. John also failed Jesus that night, but because his foundation of their relationship was first on how much Jesus loved him, even when he failed Him in the garden, he was able to step over the failure to be at the feet of Jesus at the time of His need.

John was the only disciple of the twelve who was at the cross with Jesus. The others were alone, feeling bad, and probably drowning in condemnation. While Peter was feeling unworthy and drowning in condemnation, John was at the foot of the cross because he clearly understood that his relationship with Jesus was not based on how much he loved Jesus but how much Jesus loved him.

Many people want to walk in healings and miracles or base their healing on how much they love God. A couple of years ago, I received an e-mail from a lady who asked me why she had not been healed, as she loved the Lord with all of her heart, soul, and mind. As I read this e-mail, the Lord spoke to me so clearly and said that the cross was not a demonstration of our love to Him, but of His love toward us.

Our foundation for walking in healing and miracles has to be on the basis of His incredible love that He has toward us and toward this world. I have had a few approach me to ask about Matthew 22:37. It's always important that we put Scripture into the context of who was being addressed. People have said to me that it's written in red from the words of Jesus, Himself. When we put this Scripture into context, this is how it actually reads:

> *But when the Pharisees heard that He had silenced the Sadducees, they gathered together. Then one of them, a lawyer, asked Him a*

question, testing Him, and saying, "Teacher, which is the greatest commandment in the law?" Jesus said to him, "You shall love the Lord your God with all your heart, with all your soul, and with all your mind" (Matthew 22:34-37).

Please hear what I am addressing here. I love the Lord with all my heart, soul, and mind. I love Him so dearly and would do anything for Him. My life is sold out to the purpose of releasing the realities of Heaven to earth. I am indebted to seeing Jesus receive all that He paid for, but the foundation for this must be first knowing and believing just how much I am already perfectly loved.

In this is love, not that we loved God but that He loved us....
We love Him because He first loved us (1 John 4:10,19).

In my years of ministry, I have met many people who have asked me, "Chris, I love God so much, yet why do I fail to see the power of God displayed through my life?" I love to look into their eyes and ask if they know how much they are loved. Very few look me back in my eyes and tell me how much they are loved. Many look away or look down or divert the subject. We need a greater revelation of the Father's love that He has toward us. (This is not the only reason; I will address other reasons further into this book.)

I so believe in loving God with all my heart, soul, and mind, but I can't help but fall in love when I first see just how much I am first loved. My love is the byproduct of knowing how much I am loved.

Several years ago, I began seeing the numbers 111 thousands of times a year. How many of you know that English, German, or Spanish is not God's first language? He speaks in many ways, through nature or numbers, to name a couple. I encountered these numbers so many times that it became almost scary. I knew that God was trying to highlight something to me. I regularly took flight 111, and I would take out my iPhone to check the time to find it was 1:11.

One day I was ministering in Nebraska, and I had a five-hour drive to the Denver airport. I finished ministering at 11 p.m. and had a 6 a.m. flight, so I was in for a long night. As I was being driven to Denver, I could not keep my eyes open. I kept drifting off and kept being awakened by my nodding head. At one point, I nodded, my head went forward, and I hit my head on the dashboard of the car. Then I got such a fright that I slammed into the back of the seat. I was now wide awake. I looked out the window to see a road mile marker to show that we were 111 miles from Denver. We arrived in Denver to fly to Sacramento and on arriving, I turned on my phone to see what time it was, to find it was 1:11 p.m. I said, "OK, God, what are You trying to tell me?"

I remember so clearly that He said, "I have not hidden it from you; I have hidden it for you, so keep searching." I searched every Scripture that I knew that was 1:11 or 11:1, and there are some good verses, but I knew that they were not what He wanted to show me. There were also some not-so-nice passages. Even right now as I type this, I just looked at my battery life left on my computer, and it has 1 hour and 11 minutes remaining.

Several weeks later, I said to God, "God, if You are trying to show me something in Scripture, then I have missed it. I have searched every Scripture that there is of 1:11 or 11:1."

He said, "You missed one."

I said, "No, I got them all."

He replied, "All but one. Try Mark 1:11."

I raced for my Bible to read it: "You are My beloved Son, in whom I am well pleased" (Mark 1:11).

Every time I see the numbers 111, I always take a refreshing moment to enjoy His delight that He has toward me, resting in the pleasure that I am a much beloved son.

God is no comparison to your earthly father. Your own father may have rejected you, but your heavenly Father accepts and loves you perfectly. The

Son of God, who loves you, gave Himself for you as if you were the only person who ever lived.

God does not love you for what you do. God does not love you for your service. God loves you because that is what He does; He is a God of love.

When you live out of the foundation of how much you are loved and accepted and that God is your loving Father, you will find yourself loving God back with all your heart, soul, and mind. The beginnings of the foundations will be set correctly where miracles will flow because of your identity of Him in you and you in Him.

ßß

NO OFFENSE TAKEN

When you are not correctly and securely set in the foundation that you serve a loving Father who loves you as you are and that He is the Father of acceptance and love and the giver of good things, then when life throws you a curveball, you will end up saying, "God, what are You doing to me?" We end up blaming God, as opposed to allowing the goodness of God to navigate us through the situation.

My journey came to a decision point while I was on a ministry trip in southern India. I had gone to India to participate in a healing crusade with Randy Clark. It was a warm Sunday in January 2006, and I felt that I had heard the Lord say that He wanted to do something special in the lives of children. The day started, and I had the opportunity to preach at a friend's church on the Sunday morning before the evening crusade. I arrived at the church to find that all the children had already been sent home as they had had a children's service earlier in the morning. I thought that somehow I had missed the Lord's voice, so I continued with the service. My translator had not shown up, so they asked me to share for 90 minutes until he arrived and then preach for another 90 minutes once he arrived.

I remember the day so clearly. I preached on my favorite subject, the goodness of God, and that our circumstances that we go through do not dictate the goodness of God. The preaching time was over, and God's goodness was poured out like water on a parched land. I have found that God can't help but show up when the declaration of His goodness is made. The miracles that happened that morning were simply staggering.

The blind, the deaf, and the lame were healed. We were handed a young baby who was covered in lesions all over her body from head to toe. They were deep and nasty. Right in front of our eyes, they began to dry up, and new skin began to form. We received word the next day from the mother that the baby woke up the next morning with entirely new skin, head to toe. Children began to emerge from everywhere, and the miracles and healings flowed.

Another young boy, about 13 years old, had intestinal issues. He received prayer and hit the ground under the power of God. He was out for about 20 minutes, and when he came around, he sat up and asked, "Who was the man who came and took my stomach out, cleaned it, turned it around and put it back in?" That young boy left the service that day pain free. There were many other miracles that morning and in that church of 225 people, we had counted 157 miracles. A great day in the Kingdom!

We had lunch and returned to our hotel with just enough time to change our shirts and jump onto the bus to head to the crusade, where thousands of hungry people were waiting. What I thought was a fulfillment of what the Lord had spoken to me about was only the beginning. What happened next literally shook me, and I still to this day feel the emotion of it as I write five years later. This was the last night of our crusade. The message was completed, and the ministry team was set loose to release the Kingdom on the sick and the dying. We as a team had raised $100,000 to hire trucks to go into the surrounding areas up to 30 miles away to bring many sick, dying, deaf, blind, and crippled to the meetings.

No other night of the eight crusade nights had this happened, but as I walked through the crowd, a young baby just literally ended up in my arms, almost thrown over the security barrier. The child was healed and passed back. One child after another was passed over. Some parents wanted blessing, and others needed healing for their children, and Jesus healed every one of them. An older lady, about ten deep in the crowd, caught caught my attention. She was holding a young boy, who, I later found out, was five. He was asleep in his grandmother's arms.

I asked if I could take him and hold him. "Does he need blessing or healing?" I asked.

The grandmother replied, "My grandson has never stood, never taken a step, and never walked in his life." About this time, the boy woke up and burst into tears, as he had a very white man looking down on him, but when he had gone to sleep earlier he had been in a precious Indian lady's arms. I quickly pulled every trick I knew, and the one that settled him down was M&M's. The crowd had breached the security barrier and was pushing in around me for my attention, wanting prayer. I was so moved with compassion for the boy; it seemed like he and I were the only people standing in that field that evening. I took him and my friend Carey to the front, away from the demands of the crowd.

The little boy was now my friend. (His name in English, I later found out, is translated "bright and shining light.") I told him that my friend Jesus loved him and wanted to heal him. While Carey was making friends with him, I lay in the dry and dusty soccer field so moved by compassion, then I heard the clear voice of the Lord say, "Pick him up and walk him."

I turned to Carey and told him what I had heard the Lord say, and he said, "I heard exactly the same."

I said, "Let's not think about it but just be obedient to what we both heard."

We had taught the little boy in his own language to say, "More, Jesus." We told him we were going to walk him, and we just wanted him to say, "More, Jesus." Carey took his torso, and I took his legs, and we began to walk him. To my shock, with Carey holding his torso, he just walked off saying, "More Jesus." We went to holding his arms and then his hands and then his little fingers.

I turned to his grandmother, thinking I must have misunderstood, and she was weeping on the ground. I said, "Did I misunderstand the situation?"

She said, "I already told you. He's never stood, never taken a step, and never walked." It was now past midnight, and the truck that he had come in was due to leave, and he was paged over the PA to return to his truck.

The field was almost empty, and I returned to my bus ready for the hotel. I sat in the bus overwhelmed with joy over what had just happened, and I heard the Lord say, "Celebrate by getting back on the front line." I jumped out of the bus and ran back to the soccer field and found a young lady who had not received prayer and was 100 percent deaf in one ear. I had hardly lifted my hand to her ear, and it popped open.

We returned to the hotel, and I asked Randy why it was that I prayed for 20 minutes for a crippled boy, and he was healed, yet I had prayed for my own daughter's situation for eight years at that point and had not seen breakthrough. God began to reveal to me that I was carrying an offense with God that needed to be dealt with. See, here's my own story.

My first daughter, Charlotte, was born in 1995. Within a few hours of her birth, she had a massive grand mal seizure. She was in intensive care for three weeks, and when she was about to be sent home, the neurologist took us into her office and said, "Charlotte's brain was so damaged that, medically speaking, she will never walk or function in a normal manner. The best thing that you can do for her is to take her into a loving home environment and love her the very best that you can."

Our journey began, which I believe to this day propelled me into a healing ministry, but I needed to deal with the intellectual offense that was formed toward God. Too many times we hold on to disappointments and burdens, and we wonder why we struggle to walk in a life of fruitfulness.

Over the next few years, Charlotte developed scoliosis in her spine, and in 2008, it needed urgent surgery. It twisted to 104 degrees and had affected one side of her lung, and without a miracle or breakthrough, the crushing of her heart would be only a matter of time.

> ### *How we deal with the disappointments of today will determine the fruit of tomorrow.*

In June 2008, Charlotte underwent one of the most painful operations that a person can have. She needed to have her spine fused from the base of her neck to her tailbone. The operation took eight hours, during part of which she was hung upside down, which resulted in her eyes being swollen shut for almost a week. During the operation, Charlotte lost all her blood five times over and continued to bleed after the operation for a couple of days. The doctors were at a bit of a loss, and she was monitored closely in intensive care for five days. One morning I walked into her room and closed the glass doors and curtains and started to play worship music, and I worshiped right in the face of the enemy. That day I stood there and said, "Regardless of what happens, whether Charlotte makes it through this or not, I will always declare, God, that You are good. I refuse to be offended at You, for this condition is not from You." I made a commitment to God that day that whenever I preached, I would always declare the goodness of the Lord. I worshiped with all my heart, not to get God to do something, as He's already done it.

Many times we think that God allows sickness to come upon us to teach us lessons. We then come to the conclusion that God's heart is different from Jesus' heart and, therefore, that God is warring with Jesus. While we may know that Jesus heals all our diseases, we have this mentality that God allows us to be sick, and Jesus wants us made whole, but somehow we think that this is not God's heart for us. When we hold to this theology, we create powerless Christianity, and we wonder why the Church has walked so defeatedly. The heart of the Father for His children is that we would walk in wholeness and blessings and receive all that Jesus paid for.

> *Who being the brightness of his glory, and the express image of his person, and upholding all things by the word of his power, when he had by himself purged our sins, sat down on the right hand of the Majesty on high* (Hebrews 1:3 KJV).

The phrase "express image" is translated from a Greek word that speaks of an identical copy or a perfect representation. Therefore, God's Word reveals that Jesus Christ is the identical copy and perfect representation of His Father. So we can always be confident in determining God's will concerning healing by looking at the life of Jesus.

> ### *The goodness of God is not based upon our circumstances.*

There is not one example in the gospels of Jesus ever putting sickness on anybody. So to believe that God's heart is not the same as the heart of Jesus is completely contrary to the perfect representation of Christ. He does not give sickness, and it's always His will to heal *all*. That's the good news of the gospel! Healing is in His nature; it's His name: "Jehovah Rapha."

In that hospital room, I put a chair in front of me and said, "Devil, you are going to sit in it and watch me worship." Within about two hours of my pouring my heart out in worship to God, the doctors came in to check Charlotte and confirmed that the bleeding had stopped and all the tubes could be removed.

I refuse to be offended at God. Not dealing with our disappointments and carrying burdens that were never meant for us will lead to the development of an intellectual offense with God. When I ask a crowd of people,

"Is there anyone here who has not had some level of unexplained loss in your life?" I have not yet had a person respond.

See, we have all had unexplained loss in our lives, but it is how we deal with it that will determine the fruit of what we walk in tomorrow. I am reminded of the story in Matthew 14 when Jesus found out that John the Baptist had been beheaded. Scripture tells us that Jesus went to the mountain to be alone with the Father but never made it, as the crowds pushed in needing healing. He healed the sick, walked on water, had Peter walk on water, and the crowds pushed in again for healing. He healed their sick, then finally removed Himself from the crowd to be alone with the Father.

What was Jesus doing with the Father? I would like to propose several things. First, we need to understand the goodness of the Father. As I explained earlier out of Hebrews 1:3, Jesus is the exact representation of the Father, so I believe that He was with the Father to remind Himself of the goodness of His Father. It's out of that place that we are able to minister with power and without limits hanging over our heads of whether it is the Father's will to heal or not or whether He is really good or not.

If we are going to carry burdens and responsibilities, it will only be a matter of time before the burdens on our back are too heavy to carry, and we won't want to pray for anybody else. The good news is that the burden was never meant for us.

There is one other thing that I do when I bring the burden and the glory to the cross. I take the burdens from the people who had not seen their healing manifest and use them to put fuel on my fire. I go up the mountain and get on my face before God and cry out that I must have a greater revelation of the person of Jesus Christ. I must have a greater revelation of the price that Jesus paid, and I must have a greater revelation of His grace and His goodness. I must have a greater revelation of the finished work of the cross.

Recently, I was preaching in the Midwest of the USA and was sharing out of Acts 10:38. The church that I was preaching at has John G. Lake's personal Bible. I had the joy of reading Acts 10:38 out of this Bible. It hit me afresh when I read the word "all" that I have not arrived and that every loss is a painful reminder of this.

> *How God anointed Jesus of Nazareth with the Holy Spirit and with power, who went about doing good and healing **all** who were oppressed by the devil, for God was with Him* (Acts 10:38).

When Jesus returned from the mountain after spending time with His Father, the Bible tells us that all who touched the hem of His garment were healed. I need to constantly spend time with the Father, always refreshing myself and reminding myself of His goodness, love, and grace. I cannot allow any room for an offense to come into my heart.

The easy way to determine if an offense is developing in our heart is this: If we can't learn to celebrate in the miracle of another when we need that miracle ourselves, if we end up asking, "Why them? Why not me?" then it's the start of an offense with God.

In many of the conferences I have spoken, at the time when the miracles are happening, there can be several people standing for the same miracle. One of them will get healed, and they will begin to celebrate, while the others in the room look with glumness in their faces as to why they were not. I can see it in their faces. *Why them and why not me?* When we can shift our attention to learn to celebrate in the miracle of another, we position ourselves for that same miracle. I will often say to those that have not yet received their miracle, "I want you to give thanks and celebrate with the person who just got healed, like it was your healing that you just received." When they begin to celebrate in another's breakthrough, many times their breakthrough happens right then.

Today, after dealing with the offense that was in my heart, the greatest breakthrough that I see on a constant basis is scoliosis and any issue to do with the spine. I get so excited with every miracle, as it's my platform for my own daughter's miracle. I was in a church, and three young ladies stood in front of me about my daughter's age, each with severe scoliosis. One after the other, their spines straightened, and in one case, the girl's ribs were flared. The spine moved into place along with the ribs. We must learn to celebrate, live in thanksgiving, and never be offended with God.

ENCOUNTER IN HAWAII

In 2008, I was flying to Hawaii to attend a conference. I actually went to the conference just to see the speaker, as I wanted to glean off his life. I arrived at the San Francisco airport and was waiting for my connection to Los Angeles. The flight was delayed, which meant I would miss my flight to Hawaii. At the last minute, I was transferred to the last remaining seat on the direct flight from San Francisco to Hawaii. I boarded and we departed. The man next to me was a successful businessman from Hawaii, and because of the hurry in boarding the flight, I had not realized that I had been upgraded to Economy Plus until the man asked me if I normally flew Economy Plus. I answered him that I did not even realize I had been upgraded. I asked him if he normally flew Economy Plus, and he said he normally flew First Class but on purpose had downgraded himself as the people in First Class don't like to talk much, but he liked to see what interesting person he might be seated next to.

He tried to debate me on politics. I said, "Sir you have the wrong guy. I don't even know what the Senate is."

He said, "All right, let's debate religion." I knew that God had set me up.

He asked me what I do for a job. That's my favorite question to answer. To some, I say, "I'm a physician's assistant." To others, I just say that I am a teacher, conference speaker, or writer (at that point it was just e-mails). I began to share about the miracles that I get to see on a regular basis, and he was amazed. I watched *Mr. Magorium's Wonder Emporium*, then fell asleep for a while.

When I woke, he looked at me and said, "Chris, I know why you like that movie—you believe in the miraculous." He then asked, "You say that you see miracles all the time, but my question is this, and I want an honest answer. You shared stories of people you have seen healed of stage 4 cancer and other diseases, but I want to know what you do when someone you are praying for dies?" I asked him if he wanted the short answer or the long answer. He said, "I want the short answer, but I want it honest."

I said that there were five things that I do. The first thing that I do with permission of the family is pray that they are resurrected from the dead. The second thing I do, if they are not resurrected from the dead, is bury them. Then I mourn with the family. Many Christians think that mourning is wrong. We don't mourn like the world; we mourn with the knowing that we will see them again, but we can't allow our mourning to lead us to unbelief.

The fourth thing that I do is refuse to be offended at God, and the fifth thing that I do is get up, get back on the front line and go look for the next impossibility to bow its knee to Jesus.

He looked at me intently and said, "I have never heard anything like this before. I was raised in Sunday school as a child, and I need to go home, find a Bible, blow off the dust, and read it again." The man had been in pain in his foot for 47 years from an accident. During this time, he not known life for one minute without pain. He had multiple pins in his ankle holding it together. I told him that I would love to pray for him, and he almost begged me. I wanted to see how eager he really was, so I made him wait. We landed and deplaned. I forgot my camera and needed to re-board, and he still waited. We went to baggage claim, got our bags, and walked outside, and he said, "OK, I am ready."

We sat on a sidewalk bench, and I just said a five-second prayer of releasing God's goodness. God's goodness loves to manifest with the declaration of His goodness. I said, "Move it round; test it out." I love the look on people's faces after they receive their miracle. He started slowly, and within seconds, this 60-year-old man was running around in circles on the pavement like a child, pain free for the first time in 47 years.

As I have preached a similar message, "Today's a great day for a miracle," about getting over the offenses, regardless of previous results or how many times they have been prayed for, I have never had so many people contact me to say the freedom they have personally received from this message. Many Christians have given up on ministering to the sick and dying because the burden of the loss is too hard for them to take. Use the loss to fuel your fire, refuse to live by your experience, which only pulls the gospel to a lesser level, but set the gospel as your standard, and live your life to that level. The loss is the painful reminder that we have not arrived, and weneed greater revelation of His goodness and grace.

Regardless of how many times I face what appears a defeat or how many times I get knocked down, I get myself back up and get back on the front line. I feel like Paul, sometimes: "…hard-pressed on every side, yet not crushed; we are perplexed, but not in despair; persecuted, but not forsaken; struck down, but not destroyed" (2 Cor. 4:8-9).

Live with the conviction that nothing is impossible with God. Live with a conviction that today is a great day for a miracle, regardless of how many times you have personally been prayed for. I declare over Charlotte regularly, "Today is a great day for a miracle, Charlotte." Live bold enough to pray scary prayers that He can't help but show up for. I am convinced that we will see more miracles if we step out in godly confidence, knowing that all of Heaven is waiting to back us up as we release the goodness of the Father. A few years ago, I prayed, "God, I want to see more miracles," and He clearly answered, "Well then, pray for more people." Let's go and release the goodness of the Father to this world and get Jesus all that He paid for.

———————— ⊗ ————————

CHAPTER 3

SECRETS TO GREAT FAITH

As part of my job at Bethel, I have the privilege of meeting and driving around some incredible revivalists. I always love to ask them for any insight they can give me for increased fruitfulness in my ministry. I have received some outstanding advice.

One of these revivalists was Jack Coe Junior (a healing evangelist). He taught me about the power of believing. I asked him for a key to breakthrough, and he answered, "I believe God and take God at His Word." He said that one day a reporter asked his father, Jack Coe, faith healer (1918-1956), "Jack, do you fast to get power?"

"Fast?" he answered, "No, I eat, and I believe God." I am not making a doctrinal statement on fasting. The point I am trying to highlight is that there is something powerful about believing that God is who He said He is. Jesus said to the ruler of the synagogue, "Do not be afraid; only believe."

Faith and trusting in God's nature are major keys to seeing supernatural breakthrough through your life. He healed without exception every person who came to Him. He never blessed a storm or welcomed a hurricane or an earthquake. He messed up every funeral that He ever went to, including His own.[1]

I dream of a body of believing believers who would walk in such child-like faith, trust, and confidence like Jesus walked in and not pull the Word of God to their experience, but their experience would lift itself to the standard of the Word of God.

So what is faith?

Jesus said, "When the Son of Man comes, will He really find faith on the earth?" (Luke 18:8). I pondered this Scripture for a long time and asked myself this question: Faith in what? I came to this conclusion: Faith that He is who He said He is.

How can we ever have faith in Him as the healer if we think that He puts sickness on people to teach them a lesson? How can we have faith for healing if we are not even sure if it's His will to heal? How can we have faith for healing when we look from our eyes and only see the problem? (The answer must be bigger than the problem.) I will address this later.

It's not about having faith in our faith, but about having faith that He is who He said He is. I see many who look to themselves to see if they have enough faith in themselves to produce a miracle. I choose instead to put my faith in the One who never doubts, the one whose faith is always strong, the one whose faith never wavers.

When I was a child, my father was a house builder. I can remember going to his construction sites to have lunch with him. He would ask me to help him lift some wood. See, my father was a strong man, and I was a little four-year-old. Did my father need my help to lift the wood?

Not at all, but he chose to let me help. He would ask me to take one end, and he would stand in the middle. We would lift together and move the wood to the appropriate place, and he would thank me for my effort. I would walk away feeling like I was so strong, and he made me look like the genius by saying, "I am not sure what I would have done if you were not here."

Was it really my muscle that made the difference? We tend to think that faith is purely our muscle. It was my father who really did the heavy lifting. However, I still put in the effort and would strain to lift it, but really my effort made little difference. But my effort was still required. He made me look the strong genius after we moved it. He was, in fact, the one doing the heavy lifting.

God chooses to work through us in the same manner; we put in the effort, and He produces the result. I knew that I could not lift that wood alone, but I had faith in the strength of my father and that he desired for me to co-labor with him.

The Bible tells us in Matthew 10:7-8 to "heal the sick, cleanse the lepers, raise the dead." It does not suggest we try, and it does not tell us to pray and hope that it happens. It tells us to actually heal the sick.

Have you ever worked out that what we are told to do is actually impossible? Healing is only impossible when we think that it has to do with us. It's really all about Jesus; it's about all of Him in and through all of us.

One of my favorite things to say when I speak at healing conferences—and it's fun to see the reaction on the faces of the people—is, "Christ is not the answer to your city. I am not the answer to your city; the answer to your city is Christ in you and Christ through you."

A number of people have wanted to follow me to see how I pray to achieve results. I believe that there is merit in this, as I was always taught, "If you want to be a giant-killer, then hang around giant-killers."[2] However, people are looking for the instant formula, for the magic wand or the magic way that I pray. I tell people that my prayers don't heal people, but that Jesus is the healer.

Many people have more faith in their fancy smart prayers or faith in their own faith than they have faith in Christ the healer. It's not so much about the way that we pray; it's coming with the simplicity of childlike faith that His name is Jehovah Rapha and that He is the healer in us and through us.

When we are young children, we take the word of our father. I can remember as a child I would simply believe anything that my father said I could do. When my own children were younger, they would simply believe anything I said to them and anything that I said they could do. I was never questioned; if Dad said it could be done, they believed.

It's only when we begin to mature that we begin to logically look at things in life, and we place limitations upon ourselves, as we have now moved away from the simplicity of childlike trust and faith in our father all in the name of maturity. What would the Church look like if we returned to the simplicity of childlike faith, believing that the Kingdom of God is in us and that we can do what He said we can do?

See, it's not our job to work out how a deaf ear opens or how a blind eye is opened; it's not our job to work out how someone who is riddled with cancer with weeks or days to live goes from near death to total restoration. So what *is* our job in all this? What is our part in healing the sick? Our job is really simple. It's to believe that He is extremely good at His job. The compound name of God, Jehovah Rapha, is the first time that God introduces Himself as a compound name in Scripture: "For I am the Lord who heals you" (Exod. 15:26).

It's coming back to the place of surrender and childlike faith. So how do you stay in the place of *childlike* faith? By seeing the situation out of His eyes. God does not see the arm that is missing. He sees the missing arm. Having childlike faith is understanding that it is Him in us and Him through us. See if we think that it's us, the Bible says that we can do nothing. It's about surrender. When I come in a place of surrender, I get the fullness of the Kingdom.

> *I am the vine, ye the branches; he who is remaining in me, and I in him, this one doth bear much fruit, because apart from me ye are not able to do anything* (John 15:5 YLT).

This is where the power of grace comes in. When His grace shows up, it gives us the ability to do something that we could not have done before His grace showed up. I must learn to see the situation in front of me through His eyes because faith will look the problem in the eyes and defeat it. I can't allow the problem to become larger than the answer.

HOW MUCH FAITH IS ENOUGH?

How easy it is to get consumed in wondering if we have enough faith for the miracle. Let me propose that if we wonder if we have enough faith for the miracle, then has the miracle become purely about us? I can't afford to look inward when I have a situation in front of me that needs His divine healing touch. I have found from experience that when I look inward to see if I have enough faith, I have simply taken my eyes off the answer and have placed them on myself, and when I look inward to determine if I have enough faith, I always tend to come up short of faith for the miracle that is needed.

"...God has dealt to each one a measure of faith" (Rom. 12:3). We each already have a measure of faith. According to Matthew 17:20, "...If you have faith as a mustard seed, you will say to this mountain, 'Move from here to there,' and it will move; and nothing will be impossible for you." When you received Jesus as your Lord, then the faith of God is in you right *now*. The measure of faith you received is enough to do whatever it is that you are called upon to do. Faith is not a passive resting, but an active resting.

So the faith that I have has not come from some introspective naval gazing to see if I have enough faith. I have been given a measure of faith and faith comes from hearing the Word of God. I used to think that this meant that faith came from only reading the Word of God. However, the disciples never had the New Testament to read for their daily devotions in their day, and they seemed to be full of faith. It's feeding on the *rhema* Word of God. It's feeding and reminding myself what He has done and is doing and understanding the nature of our loving Father.

"Knowing that a man is not justified by the works of the law but by faith in Jesus Christ..." (Gal. 2:16). Though this passage is traditionally translated "faith in Jesus Christ," an increasing number of New Testament scholars are arguing that this phrase involves a *subjective* genitive, which indicates the phrase could—or should—read, "Christ's faith" (the faith of Christ) or "Christ's faithfulness." The genitive suffix in Greek implies "of" or "from," so this would read "the faith of/from Christ."

> *Knowing that a man is not justified by the works of the law, but by the faith of Jesus Christ, even we have believed in Jesus Christ, that we might be justified by the faith of Christ, and not by the works of the law: for by the works of the law shall no flesh be justified* (Galatians 2:16 KJV).

This implies that we are saved because we trust in Christ's faith, or His faithfulness. He is the One who fully pleased God, who paid the price, who redeemed man, who became the curse, who defeated death. His faith—His faithfulness—has won. Jesus did all the heavy lifting.[3]

This means that on your worst day, when you're struggling to believe or when your hope burns faintly, you're not "less saved" or "less favored" or even "less pleasing." Fix your eyes on Jesus, the author and finisher—the one who started your faith and the one who finishes it. Rest in Him. He who began a good work will be faithful to complete that work in you (see Phil. 1:6).

This further means that you don't need to conjure "enough" faith to meet a condition. Jesus met every condition for you, as you. Trust in His faithfulness. In every miracle, in every work of power and grace, God is only and always glorifying "His Servant Jesus" (Acts 3:13). Jesus had so much faith in you being saved that He freely went to the cross. Peter started his epistle with these words:

> *Grace and peace be multiplied to you in the knowledge of God and of Jesus our Lord, as His divine power has given to us all things that pertain to life and godliness, through the knowledge of Him who called us by glory and virtue* (2 Peter 1:2-3).

Peter then closes his epistle with "but grow in the grace and knowledge of our Lord and Savior Jesus Christ" (2 Pet. 3:18).

The faith that I have comes from seeing Jesus in His nature, which is goodness, grace, and love, and aligning myself to ensure that I see the situation from His perspective. I want to grow more in faith and want to see believers grow in increasing faith, for the more we see Him in His goodness and grace and the greater knowledge we come into of our Lord Jesus Christ, then the byproduct will be the abundance of faith.

I choose to put my faith in Him and Him alone. My faith is not in my prayer. My faith comes from taking the time to see from His eyes. "...As He is, so are we in this world" (1 John 4:17). It's not so much how big our faith is; it's about how big our God is.

THE POWER OF THE BLOOD

We see in the story of Exodus 11 and 12 that the angel of death was about to pass over and kill the firstborn of each family.

Now the blood shall be a sign for you on the houses where you are. And when I see the blood, I will pass over you; and the plague shall not be on you to destroy you when I strike the land of Egypt (Exodus 12:13).

What an incredible story. The story tells us that when the angel saw the blood, he would pass over them. I believe that they took God at His word. I doubt that they were worried if they had enough faith for the angel to pass over them. I doubt that they wondered and cried, "I wonder if we are going to be OK. I wonder if we are going to die. I think we might be lacking some faith!" Why don't we see that? Why? Because the power of the blood was enough. Their faith was in what God had said, not in their own faith. Their faith was in the character of God and He said, "When I see the blood I will pass over." How much greater is the blood of Jesus? My faith is in Him; it's not in my faith.

I believe that it could be easy to do people an injustice by the over-emphasis of the need for faith to see miracles or extraordinary faith for extraordinary miracles. I love faith, and faith is a critical part of the life of the believer and walking in supernatural power. My point is that faith needs to be more than some mental assent or some introspective inward look to see if I have enough faith to either be healed or to be used by God in healing.

As I read through the Gospels, in every story of the people who came to Jesus, they never came and said, "Look at my great faith, Jesus. I have the faith to be healed." They came to Jesus because they saw the nature of His character. When they came to Jesus because they saw Him in His love, goodness, grace, power, and majesty, it was then that Jesus saw them in their faith. Jesus healed each one who came to Him, and once they were healed, Jesus acknowledged their faith.

The more revelation I come into about what Christ has paid for, the greater place of authority I minister out of, knowing that it's not my works, what I have done or have not done, but what Christ has done. The more I see that it's His works, the more rest I minister out of, and the more fruit I see.

Faith arises in my heart when I simply hang out with the faithful one. When I see the situation from His perspective and His eyes, I then see the answer and am not overwhelmed by the problem. I must position myself to be overwhelmed by His goodness and consistently feed myself on Him as the answer.

NOTES

1. Bill Johnson and James W. Goll, *Dreaming with God* (Shippensburg, PA: Destiny Image Publishers, 2006), 148.

2. "If you want to kill giants, follow a giant-killer!" Bill Johnson, *Strengthen Yourself in the Lord* (Shippensburg, PA: Destiny Image Publishers, 2007), 21.

3. Acknowledgment to Dr. Bryan Davenport, Heritage Church, Vancouver, Washington, for his help in assisting in the study of Galatians 2:16.

CHAPTER 4

LET'S REMOVE THE DOUBTS

Many people think that it's because of the absence of faith that we see limited results, but I believe it is more about the presence of doubts. Many of us have been raised in church under a powerless theology, built to justify the lack of results that we see. Here is an example of doubts that I found present in myself over the years and needed to work out of my life. This can be applied either to receiving healing for yourself or ministering to others in the healing power of Jesus.

THE "PERFORMANCE" DOUBT

It is easy to think that because we are not seeing healing in us or through us that we are not working hard enough for the breakthrough. The more we fail to see, the harder we try and the harder we work. The harder we work, the more frustrated we become, and the more frustrated we become, the more unbelief and doubts come into our lives.

It's not about our performance. Healing is about His performance and what Jesus has paid for. I love to tell people that healing is only difficult when we think it's something to do with us. It's not about us; it's all about Jesus in us and through all of us. If healing were about our performance and what we have done or not done, then Christ's death would have been in vain. The demand is not on you; the demand was on Christ.

When I do healing meetings, I have often had people ask if they are good enough to be healed. Grace is the undeserved favor of God. I'm so thankful for His grace because none of us deserves to be healed; that is why it's called grace.

Grace is not just unmerited favor. It is much more than that. Grace is also the supernatural empowerment in our lives—His empowering presence that brings righteousness, peace, and joy, the empowering presence of God, which enables us to do all He calls us to do and to be all that He also calls us to be.

Healing is not about our merit or works. Jesus wants us to come just as we are. "Well, pastor, I have things that are not right in my life."

I reply, "That's OK. He's still bigger than your problems. It's His goodness that will bring you to repentance." He loves us just as we are. We don't need to come cleaned up before we come to God; we come to God just as we are.

I was ministering in a country in greater Asia recently that is known for its many religions and idols. We had the most incredible evening and saw hundreds of miracles of broken bodies. I shocked a few people when I said that they could come to my God with their gods. "Come just as you are. He still loves you and wants to heal you."

We saw the most amazing breakout of extraordinary miracles, and that night we saw two deaf-mutes healed along with a boy who was born blind. I also made an altar call for salvation after the miracles and saw several hundred give their lives to Jesus. See the demand is on Jesus, not our performance. If it were because of the performance of these people, we would not have seen many miracles, if any at all.

If it were about our performance, then we would need to be perfect to receive His touch. That would leave not only most Christians out but would leave out those who don't yet know Jesus. Whether you know Jesus or not, or whether you are from another religion, Jesus still wants you healed. "But pastor, you don't know how hard and dark my city is." Friend, *it's time to let Jesus shine.*

> **If light is brighter than darkness, then darkness is not even the problem. You don't ask to turn the darkness down.**

We have just become so conditioned to seeing the darkness, but darkness is not the problem. You realize that if light is brighter than darkness, then darkness is not even the problem. You don't ask to turn the darkness down. How do you get rid of darkness? You shine your light.

Arise, shine; for your light has come! And the glory of the Lord is risen upon you (Isaiah 60:1).

Let your light so shine before men, that they may see your good works and glorify your Father in heaven (Matthew 5:16).

We are not here to reflect His glory; we are here to shine His glory because He lives in us. Let's stop trying to reflect; let's shine. "Where sin abounded, grace abounded much more" (Rom. 5:20). When we get a revelation of this Scripture, then there will be no such place as a hard place. I have a saying that I love to use: "There are easy places, and there are *really* easy places." I have found that the darker the place that I visit, the easier it is to shine. His grace comes through in even greater measure, and His goodness leads people to repentance. Others have said, "Well, I don't believe in God, or I don't even know Jesus."

My answer is simple, "He still believes in you, and He knows you."

THE "WILL OF GOD" DOUBT

Many times people might believe that it's God's will to heal the person next to them, through someone else, but not themselves.

> *Many people might not question the will of*
> *God for the person next to them, but they*
> *question the will of God for themselves.*

We see in Matthew 8:2-3 the story of a leper who came to Jesus and worshiped Him, saying, "'Lord, if You are willing, You can make me clean.' Then Jesus put out His hand and touched him, saying, 'I am willing; be cleansed.' Immediately his leprosy was cleansed."

When I am ministering to the sick, if I ever question the will of God toward the situation, I have then taken my eyes off Him. His eyes are full of compassion, love, mercy, and grace, and when I refocus back to the answer and off the problem, I hear His voice still echoing from Matthew 8:3 saying, "I am willing."

We must pray from that place that we know it's always His will to heal. If we are praying from a place that we are not sure, we will just end up ministering out of a place of lack and praying to an invisible ceiling. We are called to bring the realities of Heaven to earth, and sickness does not exist in Heaven. It's always His will to heal. God's not sitting in the heavens deciding whom He will heal and whom He will not. The decision to heal was made over 2,000 years ago when Jesus took all our sin and sickness upon Himself on the cross:

> *Who Himself bore our sins in His own body on the tree, that we,*
> *having died to sins, might live for righteousness—by whose stripes*
> *you were healed* (1 Peter 2:24).

THE "DIVINE PURPOSE OF GOD" DOUBT

This is one of the biggest areas of error in the church today. I am thankful that it is changing. Yet many still believe that there is a divine purpose of God for them to be sick. If Jesus is our role model, then there is absolutely no foundation for this belief. Sickness is not listed among the blessings of God anywhere in Scripture. Neither Christ nor His disciples ever acted as if sickness and injury might have a good or godly purpose. Scripture does not even teach anywhere that God wants to use sickness to transform a person's character or produce repentance.

I do agree that God is able to produce good things from the bad situations that He did not desire in a person's life. However, this is a long way from saying that God wanted the person to be ill or injured to help them. God, as any good father would, wants the best for His children even when they are in circumstances in life that were not His will for them.

THE "SPECIFIC TIMING" DOUBT

This specific doubt is often closely connected with the "will of God" doubt and the "divine purpose of God" doubt. It is easy to make a doctrine to justify our lack of power. Many live out of experience Christianity, and their theology is built upon their experience as opposed to what the Word of God says.

The price is already paid for the miracle that you need or for the person whom you are ministering to. The price was paid over 2,000 years ago, and that is God's timing for the miracle. Just because we do not see a miracle take place does not mean that it was not the timing of God. The work of healing is already done. Christ has already done what He's going to do; now we need to access what has already been paid for to bring the realities from Heaven to earth.

If we look at the life of Christ, He demonstrated that the timing for healing was always when people came to Him as the healer. He never sent anyone away because the miracle was not in the timing of God.

Faith has the ability to pull into today the realities of Heaven. The realities of Heaven can be released when the prayer of faith is prayed. However, in many situations because we have lowered the gospel to our experience, we have created another gospel that would say when some specific mystery time arrives, and we have pushed into tomorrow what we could have today.

Our theology has become more about the Kingdom coming as opposed to Kingdom already here. Just because we don't see a miracle happen like we expect, we push it into the category of the Kingdom that is still coming. His Kingdom is without end (see Luke 1:33), so it will keep coming, but I refuse to justify my lack of power because I did not see a miracle by pushing it into the category of His Kingdom still coming. I have to believe that there is more Kingdom available right now than we think we have. "Nor will they say, 'See here!' or 'See there!' For indeed, the Kingdom of God is within you" (Luke 17:21).

I want to get as much of Heaven here on earth as I possibly can. I do not want to get to Heaven and find that I could have had me some Heaven on earth. His Kingdom is without end, so it will keep coming.

We see in Matthew 6:10, the Model Prayer: "Your kingdom come, Your will be done." Is this purely a prayer of petition of the believer praying from earth to Heaven? What about Ephesians 2:6, "and raised us up together, and made us sit together in the heavenly places in Christ Jesus"? If we lived in the reality of this Scripture and it was not merely a doctrine, then would the Model Prayer in Matthew 6 of "your Kingdom come" become a prophetic declaration of the life of the believer praying from Heaven to earth?

Have we reduced the Lord's Prayer to nothing more than begging for Heaven to come, and not living out of the place that Heaven is in the life of the believers, who carry many of the answers to this sick and dying world inside us?

I love the supernatural, but not to the extent that I love the person of Jesus Christ. The more that I behold Him and see His life as my model that I desire to live, the more my personal experience lines up with the experience of Heaven. If you desire to have a healing ministry that emulates the life of Jesus, then just follow Jesus' model for ministry and do what you see Jesus do. He was never on a path of looking at what was wrong. He was about releasing the answer and glorifying the Father.

> *And as Jesus passed by, he saw a man which was blind from his birth. And his disciples asked him, saying, Master, who did sin, this man, or his parents, that he was born blind? Jesus answered, Neither hath this man sinned, nor his parents: but that the works of God should be made manifest in him* (John 9:1-3 KJV).

The purpose of the miracle is for His glory to be revealed. God is not revealed in our sickness. To say that God makes somebody sick to then heal them is sick and repulsive in itself.

THE "LACK OF FAITH" DOUBT

I love faith. Faith is the currency of heaven. Just like financial currency like the US dollar makes the economy turn, faith in the Kingdom is what brings the realities of Heaven to earth. It's not the lack of faith, but the presence of doubt that is often the issue. Many believe that their lack of faith is the problem. I was in a church recently and asked people to stand if they felt that it was their lack of faith that has caused them not to see breakthrough for their own sickness, or if they were desiring to see God flow through them and felt it was because of lack of faith that they were not seeing the desired results. I was anticipating only a few to stand, but to my shock over 70 percent of the crowd stood.

If Jesus is our role model for ministry, then Jesus never turned any-body away from Him because of lack of faith. The Scripture is pretty clear that there were people who came to Him with what appears to be varying degrees of faith, from little faith to great faith. Jesus always took them where they were at, and never turned anyone away; He always encouraged their faith and healed them.

We see in Mark 9:17-24 the story of the father who brings his son who is suffering from seizures to the disciples, but they failed to heal him. The father then brings the boy to Jesus and says to Jesus, "But if you can do anything…." That does not appear to be very much faith, that he even needs to question Jesus by asking if He could do anything. Jesus answers, "If you can believe, all things are possible to him who believes." Immediately the father of the child cries out and says with tears, "Lord, I believe; help my unbelief."

There had to be faith present, even if it was enough to take the boy to Jesus, but it appears that it was a pretty small amount of faith present. He said he believed but that he needed help with his unbelief. It was not the absence of faith that was his issue, even though his faith was small; it was the presence of unbelief, but Jesus still healed the boy.

We see in Matthew 8 that the leper who came to Jesus never seemed to question Jesus' ability, but he questioned His *will* to heal him. Had this man seen Jesus heal others that He never questioned His ability? Still, he questioned His will. I think that perhaps he had more faith than the father who came with his son having seizures. Yet again we see Jesus took him where he was at, affirmed his faith by saying, "I am willing; be cleansed." Immediately his leprosy was healed.

It really does not bother me in a church meeting what the beliefs of the people are. Whether they believe that God heals today or that He does not, He is still in that unbelieving believer. He's looking for an avenue out. I will talk about this more in Chapter 11. Let's get rid of our doubts and put our attention on why we should be healed. We will see so much more.

CHAPTER 5

FACT VS. TRUTH

In my journey of walking in healing power, I have learned many lessons on what I would and would not do in the future. We need to take even the hard lessons and let them allow us to grow. One of the greatest lessons I learned early on was the difference between fact and truth.

While fact is a reality, there is always a greater reality. When ministering to the sick or positioning yourself for a miracle, it is extremely easy to live in the reality of the fact that is surrounding your life.

People tend to always look toward the problem or the fact of the circumstance. I am not talking about denying the situation. If you are sick, you are sick and need healing. What I am trying to explain is that sickness is the *fact*, but the *truth* is that Jesus Christ is your healer.

> *Faith is not anchored in the realm of*
> *fact, but in the realm of truth.*

It's extremely easy to complain about the facts and to be consumed by facts of the surrounding situation and lose sight of the higher realm of truth. When people come to me for prayer, they are always so insistent that they want to tell me all about the problems they are facing; they want to tell me the facts—and all of them.

In many cases what they are actually looking for is someone to partner with them and their problem. I am not looking to partner with anybody's problem. I am there to partner with the answer: Jesus Christ. If we are not extremely careful while hearing all the facts we can easily be pulled into their atmosphere of sympathy.

I am struck by the story in the book of Jonah. In Jonah 2, we see Jonah retelling his story about his adventure in the belly of the whale. Jonah starts off by telling the reader all the facts that were surrounding him. He says they cast him into the deep waters, into the middle of the sea. He says there were billows and breakers breaking over him and he had been expelled from God's sight. Another version says, "Water encompassed me to the point of death...weeds were wrapped around my head" (Jonah 2:5 NASB).

But then Jonah's tune starts to change. Let's look at what he says from different versions:

They that observe lying vanities forsake their own mercy (Jonah 2:8 KJV).

Those who cling to worthless idols turn away God's love for them (Jonah 2:8 NIV).

Those who cling to vain idols leave behind the gracious love that could have been theirs (Jonah 2:8 ISV).

This is powerful. Is Jonah now calling the facts of the gravity of the situation—the seaweed, the billows of the sea—nothing but lying vanities and worthless idols?

It is not about denying the facts of what is in front of you. But the abundance of Heaven (faith) has the ability to look directly at the facts and defeat them. The eyes of faith can look at the facts and still believe.

It's also not that hard things don't come, but it's God's goodness and operating from the abundance of Heaven that helps us navigate through the hard things in life and not end up blaming Him.

> *Sympathy can lock a person in their problem;*
> *compassion will pull them out.*

Now Jonah 2:6-7 are the verses that I really love from this story. This is again from different versions:

> ...Yet You have brought up my life from the pit, O Lord, my God. When my soul fainted within me, I remembered the Lord; and my prayer went up to You, into Your holy temple (Jonah 2:6-7 NJKV).

> Yet hast thou brought up my life from corruption, O Lord my God. When my soul fainted within me I remembered the Lord: and my prayer came in unto thee, into thine holy temple (Jonah 2:6-7 KJV).

Verse 9:

> But I will sacrifice to You with a voice of thanksgiving, I will pay what I have vowed. Salvation is of the Lord (Jonah 2:9 NKJV).

> But I, with shouts of grateful praise, will sacrifice to you. What I have vowed I will make good. I will say, "Salvation comes from the Lord" (Jonah 2:9 NIV).

After he had been talking all about the facts of the situation, his attention began to shift to the truth and then into thanksgiving.

Directly after Jonah lifted his voice in a sacrifice of thanksgiving and declared salvation is of the Lord, the Lord spoke to the fish and it vomited Jonah out on dry ground. Notice that Jonah's breakthrough came directly after he took his eyes off the problem, looked upon God, and lifted his voice in thanksgiving. His attention was shifted to the Lord and remembering who the Lord was, and his deliverance came immediately.

We can't live in a way that allows anything to get bigger than God's presence. If we get impressed with a problem, we will begin to exalt it. When dealing with others, be careful not to also end up as a victim.

Many times we think our complaining will somehow bring the problem to a resolution. All that we are actually doing is exalting the facts to a place higher than that of the truth/answer. I'm convinced that when we complain about the problem and exalt the problem, we are actually negatively prophesying, which brings the problem into a greater reality.

I want to illustrate this by a very simple story of something that happened to me when I was flying back from an amazing ministry trip to Rio de Janeiro, Brazil. This has nothing to do with healing, but the Lord taught me a powerful lesson.

I was boarding for my flight home, and in the boarding area was a lady with a kitten in a small cage. I said to my friend that cats should not be allowed on planes and began to let go a string of complains about cats on planes. I boarded the totally packed 747-400. I was sitting toward the front of the plane, and I saw the lady enter the plane with the kitten and head down the aisle. I again went about complaining and saying, "That cat had better not sit anywhere near me. I did not pay to sit up here to be sitting next to a cat." The kitten was crying as the lady passed me and made her way to almost the back row on the plane well away from where I could hear it. I kept my string of complaints coming to my friend for several minutes. Somehow I thought that my complaining about this would ensure that the cat would be nowhere near me. The plane door was closed, and we were right about ready to push back. There was only one seat vacant on the entire plane, and that was behind me. The lady in the row behind had her jacket on it, and the airhostess asked her to move her jacket as there was a guest who was going to be moved into that seat.

My heart almost jumped out of my chest as I knew that I had been set up. I turned around, looked down the aisle and saw the lady with the cat getting out of her seat and walking toward the front of the plane. She was instructed to take the seat behind me and to place the cat under you-know-who's seat! The cat cried the entire way to the Washington, DC airport. I sat laughing at myself as I had prophesied the answer with all my complaints.

We landed in DC, and I needed to go through immigration, collect my bags, go through customs, recheck my bags, go through security, change terminals, and re-board to San Francisco.

I was in the boarding lounge awaiting the boarding call when I turned around to see the lady with the cat just a couple of people behind me in the line for boarding. I turned to my friend and said, "I like cats. I release traveling mercies and grace to that cat."

I turned around, and the lady said, "Oh, I am at the wrong gate." She left, and I never saw the cat again.

See, we complain about facts; it does nothing. We must live out of a place where we are not consumed with the problem. We must keep our attention on the truth and live out of a place where we carry the answer within us and release that answer. Facts change, but truth remains the same.

Fact is you might be sick, but the truth is that Jesus is your healer.

Fact is you might be out of money, but the truth is that Jesus is your provider.

Fact is you might feel unlovable, but the truth is that you are dearly loved!

Fact is you might have wayward family members, but the truth is that Jesus is your restorer.

> *Facts change, but truth remains the same.*

It's *knowing* the truth that will set us free. It's not just the truth. If it was just the truth, we would all be free, but John 8:32 says, "You shall know the truth, and truth shall make you free."

He is the Spirit of truth. He is not the Spirit of facts and does not bear witness to facts. Let's put our eyes on the truth and live in a place of thanksgiving. Thanksgiving increases the Kingdom.

FAITH VS. LOGIC

Faith can see the facts of the situation and still believe. We need to be careful that we don't allow logic to get in the way. It is very easy for logic to say, "How will this happen?"

There is an incredible story that is found in Luke 1: the story of Zacharias and Elizabeth. Zacharias was a priest in the temple. He was the eldest priest, and he and Elizabeth had no children. Not only was his wife Elizabeth barren, but she was now past the age of having children.

Zacharias was serving his turn in the temple one day, burning incense (which was an act of worship). A large crowd had gathered to pray outside, opening their hearts to God the best that they knew how, when an angel of the Lord appeared and startled Zacharias with a message from God.

The minute that angel showed up, Zacharias panicked. The first words out of the mouth of the angel were, "Do not be afraid, Zacharias, for your prayer is heard; and your wife Elizabeth will bear you a son, and you shall call his name John. And you will have joy and gladness, and many will rejoice at his birth" (Luke 1:13-14). We know from Scripture that this baby boy would, in fact, turn out to be John the Baptist, who was sent by God as a forerunner to tell people to repent and get ready for the great Messiah.

What prayer was the angel referring to, we might ask? Obviously, it was Zacharias' many prayers over the years for his wife Elizabeth and himself to have a child. When the angel said to Zacharias, "Your prayer has been heard," in the original language, it actually means, "The prayer that you no longer pray." So we can take from this that by this stage it is most likely that Zacharias had stopped praying and even thinking about the possibility of fatherhood.

This did not seem to matter to Heaven; his many years of praying were still on his record in Heaven. When we pray and believe with a sincere heart, our prayers rise to Heaven and stay there on our record. The more prayers we pray, the more that they collect in Heaven. We tend to think that because we have not seen an answer that those prayers have evaporated somewhere on the way to Heaven or in Heaven. They remain before God and stay on our account.

Remember when the angel said to Cornelius the Roman centurion, "Your prayers and gifts to the poor have come up as a memorial offering before God" (Acts 10:4 NIV)?

Those prayers did not evaporate. They added up until one day when God sent a special messenger to this man. There are times in life when we are seeking answers that we must learn to persevere in prayer and stand believing God and letting our prayers build up day after day until the force of our prayers simply becomes an unstoppable tide that brings breakthrough.

We see in Luke 1:18 that Zacharias raises an objection and makes known unintentionally that he apparently has not been praying for a child recently. He questions the angel and says, "How shall I know this? For I am an old man, and my wife is well advanced in years." This is a question of logic. There is a difference between asking a question of logic (unbelief) and asking a question of wanting more information. Zacharias asked a question from logic as he had given up on asking for a child for Elizabeth and himself.

Yet in the same chapter of Luke 1, we also see an angel of the Lord appear before Mary and say to her, "Do not be afraid, Mary, for you have found favor with God. And behold, you will conceive in your womb and bring forth a son, and shall call His name Jesus" (Luke 1:30-31). When Mary said to the angel, "How can this be, since I do not know a man?" (Luke 1:34), Mary was asking a question of simply wanting more information. The angel gave her more information, and then Mary said, "'Behold the maidservant of the Lord! Let it be to me according to your word.' And the angel departed from her" (Luke 1:38).

While she had asked the angel for more information, Mary chose to take God at His word. Mary did not second-guess God. She never questioned God's ability; she just wanted more information and then took Him at His word. It would be the difference between asking, "Oh, how can that be? I don't believe that," versus, "Oh, how can that be? But OK, I will take You at Your word."

Meanwhile, back to Zacharias. We might think that the angel would reply to Zacharias, "Let me tell you exactly how this is going to happen to you. God will come and empower you both and everything will just happen, and Elizabeth will bear a son." However, that's not what happened. The angel of the Lord had already declared, on God's behalf, what was going to happen, so there was nothing left to discuss.

God had spoken through the angel of the Lord that Elizabeth would bear a son, that they must name him John, and that he would be great in the sight of the Lord. But Zacharias' logic-based question provoked a strong reaction from the angel:

> But behold, you will be mute and not able to speak until the day these things take place, because you did not believe my words which will be fulfilled in their own time (Luke 1:20).

Zacharias' mouth was shut for nine months because he questioned God's ability and then allowed logic to get in the way of faith rather than just believing and taking God at His word.

We see another occasion when logic gets in the way of faith:

> Then Jesus, again groaning in Himself, came to the tomb. It was a cave, and a stone lay against it. Jesus said, "Take away the stone." Martha, the sister of him who was dead, said to Him, "Lord, by this time there is a stench, for he has been dead four days" (John 11:38-39).

Logic prevented Martha from seeing how the miracle could take place. She had allowed the stone to get bigger in her view than the answer. "Jesus said to her, 'Did I not say to you that if you would believe you would see the glory of God?'" (John 11:40). He's looking for faith that is so strong that it would be anchored in Him and His Word. Perseverance is often required in faith. We must never give up; we must not try to arrange our own solutions.

I love it when we can pull tomorrow's answers into today, and I totally believe that we can, but what happens when they don't come? We can't give up. Our job is to continue to believe that He is who He said He is. Keep believing; you know that the Lord will see you through. "If you can believe, all things are possible to him who believes" (Mark 9:23).

When things in your life don't happen the way you think they should and you don't know what to do, don't turn to logic to try and work out just how this miracle will happen. Keep your eyes anchored on Jesus, the author and finisher of faith. Persevere in a place of faith, and never let go. Keep looking into His eyes. I would rather die in faith believing God than live in unbelief.

FEELING VS. TRUST

Countless people have asked me the same question: "I don't feel anything when I pray for the sick. Is something wrong with me?" It's amazing when we get to feel or see what God is doing. Only a handful of times have I experienced the tangible power of God going through me when I have been ministering to somebody.

It's generally not the way that I am wired. I am wired to trust that He is who He said He is and live out of my conviction that I am in Him and He is in me. One person came to me almost in tears and a state of discouragement after hearing the story of another person whose hairs on their arm stood up when they knew that God was going to heal and their hands became red hot. I replied, "That's great for them, but you don't need your hands to be on fire to know that God wants to heal. You don't need your hair standing on end; you just need to trust that it's His desire to heal all and that He lives in you."

Feeling God for healing and trusting God for healing are two of the same things. I don't need to see an angel in the room to know that it's God's desire to heal somebody. I live out of the conviction that it's His desire to heal all and it's His heart to use anybody who desires to be used by God. There are more Scriptures in the Bible that refer to trusting God than there are about feeling God.

However, trusting God does not come from something that you need to try and drum up. Trust in God develops over time in understanding the nature, character and heart of God that He has toward me and toward others.

LOADED HANDS

I live out of the conviction that as believers we all have "loaded hands." The difference is whether we are a believing believer or an unbelieving believer. "Nor will they say, 'See here!' or 'See there!' For indeed, the kingdom of God is within you" (Luke 17:21).

I was teaching at a healing conference in North America, and I called out for anybody to stand who had neuropathy in any part of their body. It was a two-leveled church and a gentleman stood at the back of the church. I pointed toward him and yelled out, "Is that you, sir?" On that he fell back into his seat and then fell forward, collapsing into his hands. I sent one of my team up to the balcony to see what had just happened. A few minutes later, the man stood to his feet and began yelling out what had happened. There were so many miracles happening in the room that I could not hear him over the happy, joy-filled crowd, so I asked him to come down to the front so that we could talk.

When he got to the front of the church, he explained to me that once he stood as soon as I pointed at him, his legs and arms, which had suffered neuropathy, lit up like a Christmas tree. He was shocked. While I was looking at him in the eyes, I touched the palms of his hands, and he began to giggle, as he had not felt that feeling for around ten years. I then tapped him on the toe, and he said, "I can also feel that." That night, he went home and reported the next day that the neuropathy was a result of advanced diabetes and liver disease and also multiple sclerosis. That night he received an overhaul of his body.

As he went to bed, he removed his socks and laughed as he actually felt the sock coming off and a growth that he had had on his foot for a number of years also fell off. He got up in the morning feeling a new spring in life, showered, and noticed that even his dandruff was gone.

I live out of a conviction that the Kingdom of God truly is in the life of believers, that it is at hand (see Luke 17:21). Therefore, we have loaded hands and we need to be careful just where we point them. At all my healing conferences, 99 percent of all the miracles are done through the hands of the believers who are present. I love to get believers to lay hands on the sick people who respond to the call for prayer for a healing or miracle.

Many believe that God wants to heal people, but they don't have the conviction that He wants to do it through them. Half of the battle is trying to get their hands out of their pockets and get them on the sick person. It's stepping past theology and into an encounter with God, Himself.

I was at a friend's church recently, and just before I went into the auditorium, my friend said to me, "You know there is an entire group here tonight from the First Church of Miracles Finished 2,000 Years Ago."

I laughed and said, "They are only one encounter away from believing." Miracle time came, and one of these church members stood because of a torn rotator cuff. I asked the person next to him to lay his hands, which were firmly in his pockets, on the other man's shoulder. Finally, they came out and were placed on his unbelieving believer friend.

I was excited, as I knew that regardless of who laid hands on his shoulder, God still wanted him healed. He was just looking for a willing vessel.

I saw the man test it out, and both men's eyes went extremely wide, as he was shocked that his shoulder was totally healed. Both the receiver and the praying man could not believe what had just happened.

I love to get believers to trust God that their hands are loaded and the One who heals lives inside them and wants out, whether they can feel Him or not. He's alive and lives in the lives of believers—and He wants out.

> *When you truly believe that your hands are loaded,*
> *you will think twice about where you point them.*

I was preaching at a church in Europe one Sunday evening. I was in full swing of my message and talking about how the Bible tells us in Ephesians that we are seated in heavenly places. I went on to say that if we are seated in heavenly places, we are a conduit between Heaven, itself, and earth. If we are seated in heavenly places, we then have the opportunity to pray from God or with God from the place of abundance. I then went on to say, "So if the power of God is going to show up, who will it show up through?" I pointed my hand in the air, which was pointing at a large ceiling light, and when I said "power," there was an almighty bang in the room and all the lights in the room shut down. A flash of lighting then flew across the large auditorium right in front of me. I was in a prime position to get the best view possible.

I stood in shock, not knowing what to do. I did not know if it was the enemy trying to destroy my meeting or God showing His awesome power. I turned to my translator and said, "Do you think your voice will carry without the microphone?" He said yes, so I said, "Let's go for it in the dark." I restarted my message and said I was talking about the power of God. As soon as I said "power," the lights and sounds came back on.

We continued and had a wonderful evening, seeing many miracles. The next day I was in a neighboring country and sitting in the church gardens preparing to teach when I received an e-mail explaining that the power company went to examine what had happened and no fuse, breaker, or circuit had blown, and it was left as unexplained.

The Holy Spirit is always a gentleman, but not always well behaved.

Talk about getting a new revelation of the fear of God. This was the start of the journey of God speaking to me about believers having loaded hands. What more would we see if we actually believed that our hands are loaded with the power of the living God?

CB

CARRYING HEAVEN

When Jesus was baptized, the heavens were parted, and a voice came from Heaven and said, "This is my beloved Son, in whom I am well pleased" (Matt. 3:17). The original language for this verse refers to a violent action of the ripping of the heavens. Many believers pray week after week for God to open the heavens. Yet the heavens have already been opened, and they have never closed. We come to believe the heavens are closed because of our lack of fruitfulness.

When Jesus was beaten and hung on the cross, the price was paid in full, the heavens opened, and God, Himself, took up residence inside the believer. Out of our lack of miracles we come to the conclusion that the heavens are closed and we need to plunder the heavens and beg God to open them up.

The heavens are already open. We already carry the atmosphere of Heaven. I won't allow myself to cry out for an open Heaven as if there is something else that He needs to do. I do believe and pray that there will be a greater dimension of a coming open Heaven, but I also believe that it will come from believers arising into their identity, knowing not just who we are in Christ, but who Christ is in us.

When we realize who it is that lives in us, we can then carry and release that atmosphere. Are we thermostats or thermometers? Do we take the temperature or do we set the temperature? If we take the temperature to determine if the atmosphere is right for miracles, then we have already missed it.

I tell my Healing Room teams, "We create an atmosphere for the sake of the sick who are coming in, not for the team's sake." If we don't come ready, then we have, to a large degree, already missed it, as we should not need an atmosphere to create the miracle; the miracle creates the atmosphere.

At Bethel School of Supernatural Ministry, while teaching a class on healing, I taught out of the story in Mark 5 of the woman with the issue of blood.

> *Now a certain woman had a flow of blood for twelve years, and had suffered many things from many physicians. She had spent all that she had and was no better, but rather grew worse. When she heard about Jesus, she came behind Him in the crowd and touched His garment. For she said, "If only I may touch His clothes, I shall be made well."*
>
> *Immediately the fountain of her blood was dried up, and she felt in her body that she was healed of the affliction* (Mark 5:25-29).

Jesus told the woman to "go in peace," a phrase that appears a number of times in the Scriptures. In Acts 16:36, the keeper of the prison says to Paul, "Now therefore depart, and go in peace," which literally means to "go in peace" like you might say as a farewell as you go. In the original language, the word "in" within this phrase "go in peace" is *en*, which means "in." But with the woman with the issue of blood, the word "in" within the phrase "go in peace" in Mark 5:34 is not *en* but *es*, which actually means, "go *into* peace." So it's not "go in peace"; it's "go into peace."

Jesus was saying to go into *shalom*, step into the realm of *shalom* like you would step into a room or a house. Not only did the woman receive healing; she received wholeness. What Jesus was really saying was "go into peace and be healed," yet we see in Mark 5:29 that she was already healed. But in the original language, the phase "go in [es] peace and be healed" actually means to "go into peace and continue to be well" or "go into peace and continue to maintain your health."

Right here Jesus is telling us a key to divine health. I believe that Jesus is suggesting that the root issue of this woman's suffering was a lack of peace. Yet the woman was healed when she encountered the answer (Jesus); the root cause was addressed secondarily.

So while I was teaching these students about walking in a place of being more aware of the atmosphere that they carry rather than the atmosphere of the problem, and the way that Jesus addressed the woman by saying "go into peace," I found myself playing the part of Jesus, standing in front of a man and speaking to him like he was the woman. I paused and said, "Well, you would not have that problem," and stepped along the front row until I met the first woman and restarted what I was saying. This was on a Tuesday. On Friday of the same week, an 18-year-young student approached me to ask, "Do you want to hear a great testimony?" Well, of course I did. She said, "Do you remember me?"

I answered, "I'm sorry. I don't."

She said, "Do you remember when you were teaching on Tuesday, and you stood in front of the man in class and were talking about the woman with the issue of blood in Mark 5?"

I said, "Sure, I do."

She continued, "Then you moved along the line until you reached the first woman in the line and restarted. Well, that was me you stood in front of."

She went on to tell me that she was healed of polycystic ovarian syndrome that day. Her doctor had told her that she could never have children because of her condition. I asked her how she knew that she was healed. She said that when I stood in front of her, she just knew, and the next day in school during worship, her stomach cramped up and she got her period, which she had not had before.

The following Tuesday in class, I was sharing the testimony of the young lady. Another student in the class, who had also been told that she could never have children because she had gone through premature menopause, decided to celebrate in the other girl's breakthrough, and immediately, *her* period, which she had not had for four years, also started.

Two weeks later, at Bethel's Twin View campus, I was teaching on a Sunday night on carrying the atmosphere of Heaven and shared these two stories. A young woman came to me after and said, "I was also in that class. I was sitting next to the girl who was healed of polycystic ovarian syndrome." Eighteen months earlier, her mom had died in her arms, and she held her, believing for the resurrection of her mom. She was so traumatized by the situation that many of her body functions had shut down, but over the past 18 months, all had returned except her period. She said, "While you stood in front of the young lady in class and shared about the woman with the issue of blood, my period immediately restarted, and I needed to rush out of the class to the bathroom." I remembered her leaving the class. I just thought I had said something to upset her. She came back a few minutes later looking very happy.

The testimonies keep multiplying, and reports are still coming in about other women healed of such issues. One lady even had her period, but each month it lasted 11 days, and since that time, she has had a regular four- to five-day period. Her pain was so unbearable that she used to have migraines and vomit.

The most dramatic situation was a young lady who suffered so badly that she even contemplated suicide. She would spend multiple days in bed each month with hot wheat bags tied around her stomach, which created third-degree burns. Her periods were always 11 days, and 6 days of this were intense. She was in the class that day and since has been having almost zero pain and only five-day periods.

My favorite one was when I was in a local grocery store purchasing a salad. I picked up a Greek salad and read the label. Unbeknownst to me, a student who had been in my class was standing nearby too embarrassed to introduce herself. She also wanted a Greek salad. She had not had a period for four months, and her doctor was unable to explain why. I decided to put the Greek salad down and took another kind of salad and left the store. She stepped in and picked up the Greek salad that I had put down, and her period restarted.

At the time of writing this book, the count of known testimonies from ladies who have been healed of issues of blood has reached 34. I have not prayed for one of them. It is just being aware of who He is that lives in me and living out of the place of abundance, knowing that I carry Heaven.

The more that I use faith to recognize the One who lives in me, the more I get to experience what I call accidental healings. One man I walked past approached me and said, "Do you know that you heal people when you pass them?"

I smiled and said, "Well, I kind of have an idea that something is up." He shared that he suffered from intense pain from prostate cancer, and when I simply passed by, all the pain immediately lifted. I saw him several days later, still pain free.

On another occasion, in Redding, I just shook a man's hand to greet him, and he later told me, "So, you know that you heal people when you touch them?"

"Why?" I asked. He had an abscessed tooth for three days, and as we shook hands, it cleared and never gave him trouble again.

I dream of a body of believers aware that they are full of the atmosphere of Heaven. I dream of a body of believers so full of Heaven that miracles would happen without their even realizing it. I dream of a body of believers so full of the confidence of the One who lives in them that miracles would become a common, daily event. I had a number of people ask me if I felt anything when I stood in front of the first young lady. I felt nothing at all. I was just teaching the Word of God in a class, and we were not even going after miracles.

In my spare time, I am doing some study outside of the church. I was attending a three-day block class out of state, and our teacher, whom I had not met, went around the room asking us to introduce ourselves and state what we do for a profession. I turned to my friend I was with and said, "I'm not saying that I'm a pastor, as I will get cold-shouldered the rest of the class."

He said, "You'd better think fast then. You are next."

The teacher pointed at me and said, "Your turn."

I stood and said, "My name is Chris Gore. I am originally from New Zealand but now live in Redding, California, and I'm a public speaker and an author."

> *When we are conscious of who we are and who lives in us, then we carry and release what we are conscious of.*

The final day of the class came, and I was packing up to leave five minutes early, and the teacher saw and stopped me and said, "Chris, I need to see you in private. Can you wait for a few minutes?" The class finished, and she took me out into a hallway, looked me right in the eye and said, "I want to know who you really are and what you really do." I asked why, and she said, "There is something about you and on you that I saw the first day you walked into the class, and I liked what I saw, and I want to know what it is." She went on to say that she had never seen it before on anyone and wanted to know what I really do. I got to share with her what I do and the privilege that I have each day to release the reality of Heaven that lives inside us. I shared a few testimonies of what I have gotten to see. She looked at me and said, "I knew there was something different about you."

She said teachers are not allowed to ask for students' e-mails, but added, "I want your e-mail, as I want to know more."

How much of the answer are we aware that we carry? Many believers are looking for God to show up as if He's out in orbit somewhere, but they fail to live out the reality that His dwelling place is within them.

> *To them God willed to make known what are the riches of the glory of this mystery among the gentiles: which is Christ in you, the hope of glory* (Colossians 1:27).

Carrying confidence in God that we are His dwelling place is a key part of walking in a supernatural lifestyle. We must carry a confidence that God wants the person we are praying for healed and whole, even more than we want to see them healed and whole. We are so wired to see before we believe, but we should believe and when we believe, we will see.

There's a fascinating story in Mark 11, when Jesus and the disciples had come out of Bethany, and He was hungry. They saw a fig tree and went to see if there was anything to eat off it. They found nothing but leaves, for it was not the season for figs. In response Jesus said to it, "Let no one eat fruit from you ever again," and His disciples heard Him (Mark 11:14).

Now the next morning, as they passed by they saw the fig tree dried up from the roots. This is the point that gets me. Peter looked at the tree and appeared shocked. "Rabbi, the tree you cursed has withered away."

"And Jesus answering saith to them, 'Have faith of God'" (Mark 11:22 YLT). Jesus goes on to say that when you pray, believe that you receive what you pray for, and you will have it. (See Mark 11:24.)

Peter seemed shocked that the tree was dead, but Jesus did not seem shocked at all. Peter needed to see the dead tree before he believed, but Jesus believed before He even saw the dead tree. Jesus spoke what He wanted to see. Jesus saw it well before Peter saw it.

It does not say in Mark that the tree died and withered instantly. It was not until the next day that they found the tree dead. Jesus walked in so much heavenly confidence that He just believed that when He cursed the tree, it was as good as dead.

I can't help but wonder how many times we have prayed for someone with cancer and not seen a result, then didn't believe because we did not see. Yet the fig tree's leaves did not fall off immediately, but surely the roots of that fig tree were killed the moment that Jesus cursed it, and it took until morning for the leaves to fall off and the branches to wither.

> *Jesus never told us how to address unanswered prayers, as He walked in an unlimited certainty and confidence that His prayers were always answered.*

What if we believed that when we prayed for cancer that the root of that disease was dealt with and the housing of the cancer (tumor) just needed time to respond to the dead root? There has not been one person I have prayed for with cancer that I knew for sure that they were healed on the spot. In all cases, I needed to believe that the root was dealt with, and the body then recovered over time. I then hear later on after the person has gone back to the doctor that the cancer is gone, and the body is in rebuilding and recovery mode.

You might be saying, "Yes, but that is Mark 11:12. What about the same passage in Matthew 21:19, where it says, 'immediately the fig tree withered'?" I am always going after the immediate and instant miracle. But I also know that there are many conditions that can't be verified immediately and can only be verified by additional testing from a doctor. What is important is that we continue to receive even after someone prays.

Shelley came to see me to tell me of her amazing testimony that supports the point I am trying to address. This is written unedited as a first account testimony.

Approximately three years ago, I suffered with chronic cystic ovaries. The cysts were hard cased, several were filled with blood, and they seemed almost like tumors. They ranged in size from 3/4 inches across to 3 inches across and there were several on each ovary. They were quite painful and would leak fluid and blood into my abdominal cavity, causing inflammation and irritation. After discussion with my doctor on my options, it was determined that the best course of action would be a total hysterectomy (removal of ovaries and uterus). My preoperative appointment was then scheduled.

Our family lived about an hour and a half drive from Bethel Church, but we consistently drove to Bethel to attend church. (We are now permanent residents of Redding). Three weeks before my pre-op appointment, I went forward for prayer at Bethel regarding my medical condition and met a lovely couple who were prayer ministers. They were very encouraging and diligently prayed for me until they felt that something had shifted. The pain had reduced by about 80% and I was very grateful, but I could tell the cysts were still there as my tummy was still swollen. Three weeks later I was attending my pre-operative visit, and the doctor decided to do an ultrasound on my abdomen and discuss the details of the surgery with the cysts on screen. I was lying on the examining table and could clearly see the ultrasound screen with the doctor and the nurse assistant. The doctor began by measuring the first cyst that appeared on the screen, and we began dialoging about the surgery.

Suddenly I felt a light, feathery sensation inside my abdomen. At the same time the image on the ultrasound screen became completely fuzzy. The doctor and the nurse became alarmed. The doctor stated, "The machine is malfunctioning," while the nurse lunged at the machine and began adjusting knobs. The image began to reappear on the screen and the cysts could be made out when suddenly, the cysts dissolved and vanished! The doctor was frantically running the ultrasound wand over my abdomen, the nurse was still adjusting knobs, and I was staring at the screen in dumb shock. All of my internal organs appeared back on the screen exactly where they should be, but there were no cysts to be found. After the doctor and nurse examined and reexamined my abdomen in silence, the doctor finally let his arms drop to his side and said, "Your surgery is cancelled...there is nothing wrong with you" and walked out of the room. I am happy to report that the symptoms have not returned.

I love the story in Mark 5 of Jesus raising the daughter of Jairus, the ruler of the synagogue, from the dead. I have preached from this story a number of times, and it's one of my favorite stories. Let's read the passage:

While He was still speaking, some came from the ruler of the syna-gogue's house who said, "Your daughter is dead. Why trouble the Teacher any further?" As soon as Jesus heard the word that was spoken, He said to the ruler of the synagogue, "Do not be afraid; only believe." And He permitted no one to follow Him except Peter, James, and John the brother of James. Then He came to the house of the ruler of the synagogue, and saw a tumult and those who wept and wailed loudly. When He came in, He said to them, "Why make this commotion and weep? The child is not dead, but sleeping." And they ridiculed Him. But when He had put them all outside, He took the father and the mother of the child, and those who were with Him, and entered where the child was lying. Then He took the child by the hand, and said to her, "Talitha, cumi," which is translated, "Little girl, I say to you, arise." Immediately the girl arose and walked, for she was twelve years of age. And they were overcome with great amazement (Mark 5:35-42).

When I had previously preached about this story, it was always from the perspective that Jesus had put everyone outside of the house to protect His atmosphere of faith that He carried. While I think that there may be some merit in this, and it is sometimes necessary, I don't believe that is why Jesus put the mourners outside. I was flying home from a ministry trip, and I felt like the Lord had said to me, "What you just preached was wrong."

I said, "What part?"

He said, "The part about Jesus putting the mourners outside to protect His atmosphere of faith."

I asked what was wrong with that. I felt the Lord say in a very clear way, "Well, that's for you to search out." My flight had just been delayed seven hours, as the pilot had not shown up. So I guessed I had time to begin my research. This is what I discovered, which changed the way that I now preach this message.

In my studies, I found that mourners in the day of Jesus were often hired, professional mourners. They would come and weep and mourn over the dead. It makes me wonder if they even actually knew the girl's name. One minute they were supposed to be in deep mourning, and the next minute they were laughing and ridiculing Jesus. Jesus walks in and He says:

> *"Why make this commotion and weep? The child is not dead, but sleeping." And they ridiculed Him. But when He had put them all outside, He took the father and the mother of the child, and those who were with Him, and entered where the child was lying.*

So why did He permit no one to follow Him except Peter, James, and John? Why did He kick the mourners out? Was He protecting His atmosphere of faith?

I would like to propose that Jesus walked in such confidence of the Father and the backing of the atmosphere of Heaven, that He simply knew before He even got there that the mourners would not be needed. He knew that it was not going to be a time of mourning, but a time of rejoicing. He knew He was not going to a funeral service, but to a resurrection party.

> *Do we approach the enemy to see what the atmosphere is like? If we do and we don't like it, it's quite likely that we have already missed the miracle.*

Jesus never walked in the house to take the temperature of the room to see if it was the right atmosphere for a miracle. He walked in there ready to set His own temperature, because He was not a thermometer but a thermostat. Jesus was His own weather system.

As you go into situations, go with the mindset that all things are possible. Walk in the confidence that the Spirit that raised Christ from the dead lives in you. (See Romans 8:11.) When you become so aware of the answer that lives in you, the problem will pale into insignificance. When you are filled with the confidence of His character, then you can't help but carry and release the atmosphere of Heaven all around you, sometimes without even knowing.

---------- ○ ----------

CHAPTER 7

HIS GRACE AND OUR EFFORT

While I stress the importance of ministering out of rest, I am not talking about sitting back and doing nothing. Kingdom rest is not the absence of activity. I have seen people who so want to see God use them in extraordinary ways through healings and miracles, but they seem to think that God is somehow going to sovereignly heal people through them without their having to lift a finger.

I can ask them the question, "Well, if you want to see breakthroughs, let me ask you how many people you are praying for?" Many come up with excuses and now wonder just why they are not seeing miracles by their hands. Many seem to have a distorted view of "It is finished," meaning they think that all the work is done and there is nothing left for us to do. The work has only just begun. The Kingdom of Heaven is not in us to do nothing. The Kingdom of Heaven is in us so that we can use the power that is within us to defeat the powers of darkness here. There is no point waiting until we get to Heaven before we use them; there will be no need for them there.

So much of the grace message today leans toward the side of God's sovereignty and promotes a lazy Christian life. While Jesus has done the heavy lifting, there is still an effort that is required by us to see His King-dom come right here on earth. A number of stories in Scripture illustrate that without making an individual effort, the people involved would have missed their day of visitation with Jesus. I am not talking about works or our merit.

We see in Luke 18:18 the story of the rich young ruler approaching Jesus and saying, "Good Teacher, what shall I do to inherit eternal life?" This young ruler approached Jesus as a teacher of the law, and Jesus addressed him back with the law. The young man tells Jesus that he has fulfilled all these things. He approached Jesus from the perspective of his personal works and merits to try to earn salvation.

Now he is told that he needs to go and sell all that he has and give it to the poor, and we are told that he went away sorrowful, for he was very rich. Religion is just this way. There is always one more thing that you must do. This rich ruler did not receive eternal life that day because of his works mentality and own merit mentality. His approach was, "What must I do?" That does not mean that we get to sit back and do nothing without effort.

Last year, I studied the story of the rich young ruler in Luke 18 and also the story in Luke 19 of Zacchaeus. I gave my interns an assignment to find total opposites or comparisons between the two stories. It is a wonderful assignment to do in studying the Word of God. Together they came up with 30 opposites or direct comparisons.

When we look at the story of the Zacchaeus, we discover that he is also a rich man, but the outcome of the story is very different. Zacchaeus received salvation, but his approach to Jesus was rather different from that of the rich young ruler.

And he sought to see who Jesus was, but could not because of the crowd, for he was of short stature. So he ran ahead and climbed up into a sycamore tree to see Him, for He was going to pass that way (Luke 19:3-4).

While Zacchaeus did not approach Jesus in a works and merit mentality, effort was still required of him for his day of visitation. He still needed to run ahead and climb the sycamore tree. The woman with the issue of blood in Matthew 9 still had to push through the crowd to touch the hem of Jesus' garment to receive her miracle.

Those who say that because we are under grace, we don't need to do anything are promoting and creating lazy Christianity. There are often two camps of believers: those who emphasize faith (our part) and those who emphasize God's grace (His part). Often those who emphasize grace believe that everything is up to God, that He can and will do exactly whatever He chooses.

If we take this extreme, then everything is up to God; therefore, we don't even have a role to play, as it's entirely about His sovereignty. If it's totally about His grace and His sovereignty, then why does He need us? He will save and heal whom He wants to save and heal. When we take this approach, we will end up blaming God for everything that ever happens to us. Why even believe in God for anything? Why even pray for anyone? The gospel that was good news to the sick and dying is now dependent on how God is feeling today.

Then there are those who teach faith to the degree that it puts people in bondage because faith in itself can become law. We then need to jump through hoops, and when we don't see the desired results, it's because we missed a hoop or a requirement and now find that we are back at square one trying to perform again.

I love faith and I love grace, and both faith and grace need to be present to be able to see the power of God released through our lives. It is not grace without faith. Some believe that it's all about only His grace, and they rest in that, and see nothing. Yet others think it's all faith and no grace. It must be both, not a striving action, but an action out of rest. Faith is not passive, but active. Faith is empowered by grace.

Faith will appropriate what God has already provided by His incredible grace. And it can't be faith without His grace because faith is by His grace. Don't get me wrong; we do not need to come before God and act like a beggar, begging God to do something. God by His incredible grace has provided everything. Our part to play is to trust and rest that God has already done it and see Him in His grace. It is then that faith arises in me and knowing it's not my merits or works but by His unmerited favor that He chooses to use me.

When you truly get a revelation of the pure grace of God and His love for you and for others, you will be compelled to give Him away. You will find yourself making efforts and taking risks like you have never done before. Why? Because lovers make better workers! I know that the greater the revelation that I come into of His love, goodness, and grace and the knowledge of the person of Jesus Christ, the more effort I make to see His Kingdom come right here on earth.

I am so smitten by His nature of love, grace, goodness, tenderness, gentleness, and kindness that I am compelled to give the world an encounter with His love. I simply can't sit back and do nothing on the grounds of Jesus' final words on the cross, "It is finished." (See John 19:30.) We were born to be loved by God, to love God, and to love others around us. We were born to be transformers of families, workplaces, cities, regions, and the nations of the world so that we would see Jesus receive the full reward of His suffering.

⊗

CHAPTER 8

THE POWER OF THANKSGIVING

Thanksgiving is such an important key in the Kingdom. I must learn to keep myself postured in a place of thanksgiving for everything that I get to see. Whether I am the one praying or I am the one receiving, thanksgiving always increases the Kingdom in my life.

One of the biggest challenges that I have encountered in ministering to people is to get them to focus on what has happened as opposed to what has not happened yet and to give thanks for the small things. People can tend to be unthankful. I love to give this illustration: let's say that someone comes for healing, and they have a frozen shoulder that is so frozen it is stuck to their leg. So they receive prayer and are asked to check it out. Let's say that they can now move it four inches off their leg. Nine times out of ten, their reply would be, "But I still can't lift it up." They receive prayer a second time, and they can now move their arm to their shoulder height. It astonishes me that they still reply, "Yes, but I still can't lift it over my head." See the importance of putting our attention on what has already happened and not on what has not? I would normally say at this point, "Don't focus on what has not happened, but place your focus on what has happened, and give thanks for that, and we will pray again out of a place of thanksgiving." It's normally about then that they get it, and they see the remainder of the miracle manifested in their life.

A couple of years ago, I was ministering to a young lady (about 15) who had broken her jaw in an accident. During the reconstruction surgery, the surgeon slipped with a device and severed the lingual nerve to her tongue. The lingual nerve is the nerve that supplies sensory innervations to the tongue. She had lost speech and needed to learn to talk again with the help of speech therapy. She underwent two additional surgeries in which the surgeon attempted to repair the severed nerve, and not only were both surgeries a failure, but they also made the problem worse, causing her to have a hyper-sensitivity to particular foods. She could not taste any foods, but if she ate a strawberry, her head would scream in pain.

She came for healing, hands were laid on her jaw, and she received prayer. Nothing happened at first, so she received prayer again. The second time nothing happened, so she received prayer a third time. She was asked if anything was happening, and she replied that she felt a small tingle in her throat area. She was then asked if that tingle was normal. She said no; she had never felt that before. She was told about the importance of thanksgiving and asked to put her attention on the tingle in her throat and give thanks for what was happening. She lived about 30 minutes from the church, and while her mom was driving her home from church, she was giving thanks and then began to scream as her tongue was totally restored. She had great delight in coming the next morning to inform us that for the first time in several years she could taste her food and could feel her tongue. I had the joy of meeting her mom again about 12 months later and to hear that she was still fully restored and enjoying the taste of food again.

THANKSGIVING BECAUSE OF THE CROSS

When ministering to someone, I am looking for the slightest change in their body, whether they are feeling heat, cold, or a slight improvement. I will tell them that if they feel any change, to stop me in my prayer. I then switch to thanksgiving, as the Kingdom always increases with thanksgiving. At what point does the miracle actually happen? Does it happen when heat is present? Does it happen when they can begin to move a body part that did not previously work, or did it happen at the cross when Jesus took all our sickness and infirmities? So we could even be novel enough to give thanks for the cross and what was paid for right there.

A life of thanksgiving must be a critical part of our lives. Yet many wonder why they do not see the breakthrough that they desire through their prayers. We must learn to steward what we have seen and live in a place of continued thanksgiving. I have seen many people who see a measure of small miracles, but in their zeal to see the greater works, they are no longer thankful for the little headache that got healed; they are just after the people with missing limbs.

We simply can't despise the day of small beginnings. (See Zechariah 4:10.) It's about giving thanks and living in awe for even the small things that we get to see. By living in thanksgiving for even the small things, we position ourselves to usher in the larger miracles into and through our lives.

I love the song that we sang many years ago:

> *Give thanks with a grateful heart,*
> *Give thanks to the Holy One,*
> *Give thanks because He's given Jesus Christ, His Son.*
> *And now let the weak say, "I am strong,"*
> *Let the poor say, "I am rich",*
> *Because of what the Lord has done for us.*

I was sharing in a conference about the power of thanksgiving, and I mentioned it in the context of financial breakthrough. I said, "Let's say that this man in front of me is in need of a financial breakthrough of $50,000." I walked up to him and put one cent in his hand. "He has a choice right now. He could say, 'That's hardly going to contribute toward what I need;

I need $50,000, not one cent.' The alternative is that he could recognize it as the start of his needed breakthrough and give thanks." I lifted the microphone to his mouth and said, "So what are you going to do?"

He said, "Thanks, Jesus, for the one cent. Thank you so much."

I then took a one-dollar bill and placed it in his hand. Now that's a 100 percent increase, yet so far from the $50,000. He gave thanks again. Unaware of any of his personal circumstances, I was just trying to illustrate a point.

We broke for a two-hour lunch. On his return, he walked in with his eyes large and an incredible smile on his face. He had recently married and was in need of a financial breakthrough. He went to his parents' house for lunch. His parents had had their house on the market for a number of years with no success. His parents had agreed to give him a portion of the profits from the sale of the house, which was to equal over $50,000. The market had been so hard in this country that nobody had even viewed the house in a long time. Over lunch, a realtor came with a prospective purchaser, who agreed to purchase the house there and then for cash, and a contact was signed. I don't see that as a coincidence. The power of thanksgiving is incredible.

Many people do not even think that they have anything to give thanks for. Take a breath; you can give thanks for that. You can give thanks for God giving His only son, Jesus! Thanksgiving will increase the breakthrough in and through your life.

CHAPTER 9

— C３ —

THE POWER OF HUMILITY

Walking in humility is one of the most powerful lessons that we can learn, allowing ourselves to always stay positioned to understand that it's all by the grace of God. Even on our extremely best day when faith appears to be flowing out of us, it is still by His grace.

> *"True humility is not thinking less of yourself, it is thinking of yourself less."* —C. S. LEWIS

Our identity of being in Christ and having Christ in us is so critical to walking in a life of power and understanding that we carry the authority of the Father. He's our Father, and we are His children. My concern is that we can begin to act like an orphan who has been given the authority of the Father, as we begin to step aside from the fact that it is by His grace. We can very easily begin to act out of a spirit of entitlement, thinking that we deserve to be healed or for healing to flow through us into others.

Grace is the unmerited favor of God. None of us deserves anything, but that is the power of grace. Let me try to explain through a powerful Bible story in Matthew 15:21-28.

But first I need to add some historical background to this story. Jesus is referred to 17 times in the New Testament as the "Son of David." But I guess we could ask how Jesus can be the son of David when David lived almost 1,000 years before Jesus appeared on the scene as a man. We see in Second Samuel 7:14-16 that the answer is that Jesus Christ the Messiah was the fulfillment of the prophecy of the seed of David.

Jesus was the Messiah who was promised, which means He was the seed of David himself. The book of Matthew gives us the genealogical evidence that Jesus, in His humanity, was a direct descendant of Abraham and David through Joseph, who was Jesus' legal father. Luke 3 gives us the lineage of Jesus through His mother, Mary. Jesus is a descendant of David by adoption through Joseph, and by the blood though Mary. So calling Jesus the "Son of David" refers to His Messianic title as the Old Testament had prophesied concerning Him.

> Yet the Lord would not destroy Judah, for the sake of His servant David, as He promised him to give a lamp to him and his sons forever (2 Kings 8:19).

We see here that David was promised that one of his offspring would rule forever. Jesus was called the "Son of David" while He was here on earth. Jesus was born in David's city, Bethlehem. The New Testament refers to Jesus as the "Son of David" 17 times and in the book of Matthew the title of the "Son of David" was used by various people six times. This was a Messianic title. This was a title that the Jews were able to use to address Jesus.

Now let's go back to the story in Matthew 15:21-28. I have read this story many times, but sometimes we have to read a Scripture like we have never read it before and take the time to study the context and the meaning. We see the story of the woman from Canaan who cried out to Jesus, saying, "Have mercy on me, O Lord, Son of David! My daughter is severely demon-possessed" (Matt. 15:21). Now, this lady was not a Jew; she was a

Canaanite woman from the region of Tyre and Sidon. Though she was a Gentile woman, she approached Jesus as if she were a Jew, calling him the "Son of David."

Verse 23 says that "He answered her not a word." This is the verse that I never understood until I understood the context and location of the verse. Why did Jesus answer her not a word? Did she approach Jesus in an extremely presumptuous manner? Was she trying to impress Jesus? She is a foreign Gentile woman living in a Jewish land, yet she pushes through the crowd, gets past the disciples, and calls out to Jesus by His Messianic title which was not fitting for a Gentile to call Him. Did she approach Jesus pretending that she was a Jew to show that she deserved to have her daughter healed? The story continues:

> And His disciples came and urged Him, saying, "Send her away, for she cries out after us." But He answered and said, "I was not sent except to the lost sheep of the house of Israel" (Matthew 15:23-24).

We can see from these verses that Jesus must have identified that she was a Gentile and not a Jew by saying He was sent only for the Jews.

Now we see a change in the heart of the Gentile woman. She seems like she has moved from acting out of a spirit of entitlement or presumption or coming to Jesus in her own merits, acting like she deserves what she needs. She now comes and worships Him, saying, "Lord, help me!" (Matt. 15:25). That's a big difference.

Now comes another test and an amazing lesson for us all on grace and faith: "But He answered and said, 'It is not good to take the children's bread and throw it to the little dogs'" (Matt. 15:26).

In Jesus' day, the Jews referred to the Gentiles as dogs, which was an extremely derogatory term, and even today in many parts, the Gentiles are still looked down on by the Jews as a less holy people. But what we see here is that Jesus does not call her a *dog*, but actually calls her a "little dog." It's pretty clear that Jesus pointed at her attitude, yet He softened the rebuke of her attitude by calling her a little dog, which in the Greek is actually more of an affectionate term. The Gentile woman responded with an incredibly humbling, faith-filled answer to Jesus, which is what brought her the victory.

> *And she said, "Yes, Lord, yet even the little dogs eat the crumbs which fall from their masters' table." Then Jesus answered and said to her, "O woman, great is your faith! Let it be to you as you desire." And her daughter was healed from that very hour* (Matthew 15:27-28).

We can't come to Jesus acting like we deserve His grace or deserve His healing. To really put her in a place of understanding undeserved grace, He says, "It is not good to take the children's bread and throw it to the little dogs." And she said, "Yes Lord, yet even the little dogs eat the crumbs which fall from their masters' table."

She is not now coming to Jesus on the grounds of presumption or entitlement. She is not now coming to Jesus on the grounds of her own merits or her own works. She is coming on the grounds of Jesus' grace, which is undeserved favor. She is looking at His greatness and grace, not her own greatness, works, or merit. It is then that Jesus answered her cry, healed her daughter, and acknowledged her great faith.

Healing is the children's bread. We have full access to what He has paid for. We are fully entitled to the bread and all that Jesus has paid for by the finished work of the cross as we are His children (see 1 John 3:2). We just don't need to act like orphans, demanding our entitlements and coming on the grounds of presumption or our merits. The feast is fully paid for, and that humbles me that I have access as a child of God, that I can just come as I am before Him without pretense and have full access to all that He has.

We don't need to wait for some sovereign move of God to heal us. God is waiting on us to receive the revelation that healing is the children's bread. The table is set and the food prepared. Come just as you are. It's fully paid for.

He wants us to come exactly as we are. I have often seen people come with a mindset that they don't deserve to be healed since the condition they have may be their own fault. Let's say they have lung cancer because they have smoked or diabetes from not looking after their bodies. They come as if they are not good enough to be healed, thinking maybe they kind of deserve the disease or the condition that they have. Are we then really coming on our merits and behaviors? We have each done silly things in our lives, but that again is the power of grace. Jesus just wants you to come just as you are. We don't need to be cleaned up to come to Him; we can't come before Him based on our merits or lack thereof; we just need to come in humility, and that is a wonderful platform for the power of Jesus to flow in us and through us.

> *Acknowledging God's grace might be one of the greatest signs of healthy humility.*

"...God resists the proud, but gives grace to the humble." Therefore humble yourselves under the mighty hand of God, that He may exalt you in due time (1 Peter 5:5-6).

The story of the Gentile woman is an incredible story of faith and grace. In my role as Director of Healing Ministries, I see many people who come for healing acting like they deserve to be healed, like it's their right. While it is the right of the believer because it is what Jesus has purchased for us, we can't come with a spirit of entitlement because if we are not coming with a heart toward His grace, are we then coming upon our own merits? If we are coming in our merits, did not Christ die in vain? People come with faith, but even our very faith is by the power of His grace.

That is what makes the gospel so powerful. That is what makes God's grace so powerful. Not one of us deserves to be healed. We just need to come to Jesus as we are and stop acting like we deserve it, stop pretending that we are what we are not, but recognize Him in His incredible grace. When we come seeing Him in His grace, in His merits, and in His goodness, we end up getting everything that we need. "Do not fear, little flock, for it is your Father's good pleasure to give you the kingdom" (Luke 12:32).

Recently, I was flying within another country on a ministry trip and I had the joy of taking my daughter Sophie with me. I have access into the airline's club lounge because of my mileage status with the airline. In order to be allowed inside the lounge, you need to place your boarding pass on a scanner. If the light turns green you have access to the lounge. If the light turns red, access to the lounge is denied.

I entered the club lounge with Sophie right behind me. I put my boarding pass down and the light turned green. She put hers down and the light turned red because she does not have the same airline status as I do. The attendant did not even take a second look at her red light, as she saw that my daughter came into the lounge based on my merits.

Sophie was able to come with full confidence into the lounge because she was with me, her father. She was not restricted to what she could eat, while I got to enjoy the buffet of food and drinks. Sophie had total access to all of the privileges that I had access to. But, she had no access privileges to the lounge outside of being with me.

As I pondered this, I was overcome with a fresh understanding of God's unmerited favor. If Sophie had shown up at the lounge without me and said, "Do you not know who I am?" she would have been promptly removed by security. Similarly, when we come in an arrogant spirit of presumption and entitlement. But when we come to God in a spirit of humility, realizing that it is not by our own merits but by the merits of our Father, we actually have full access to everything that is in the Kingdom. Like Sophie, we don't need to beg to gain access to the Kingdom. We can come just as we are, knowing that we have full access to the Kingdom by our Father's merits made possible through Jesus' payment on the cross.

When we are not afraid to take our place, it is then that God can take His place in our lives. When we come in the place of emptiness, it is then that we receive His fullness. I am not talking about coming in a false humility and saying, "I'm so unworthy to be healed or to be used by God." That's an extreme that will not get you advancement in the Kingdom. I spend so much time with people who have come believing a lie that they are so unworthy, that God could not and would never use them, and they feel that they are not worthy enough to be healed. That condition of the heart needs to be healed. That is a lie of the enemy. We are His masterpiece, and while we might not deserve healing by our own merits, that is the power of His grace. The spirit of unworthiness needs to be broken off the church. We will never see Jesus get His full reward with this kind of mentality. James 4:6 reads, "But He gives more grace. Therefore He says: 'God resists the proud, but gives grace to the humble.'"

We are here to glorify and lift up the name of Jesus. I want to always be giving Him the glory that He deserves and living a life of thanksgiving, living a life always giving Him the glory for every miracle that I have the joy to be a part of because it's not my power or godliness that created the miracle.

"Blessed are the poor in spirit, for theirs is the kingdom of heaven" (Matt. 5:3). The foundation of my identity is knowing who I am in Him and who He is in me, and I continue to push in for more and more revelation and understanding on this. I believe that we can have an idea of our identity as King's kids, and we can act out of authority and know all that He has for us is ours, but it comes not out of demanding self-righteousness or grabbing like an orphan, but out of surrender. The more I learn to surrender, the more of the fullness of the Kingdom I see displayed through me. The more I learn to rest in His grace, the more the power of God flows through me. It's grace and faith together; it's not one without the other.

It is such a joy to be used in power by God, to get to see thousands of miracles each year and see lives that were so tormented set free by His Kingdom in me. But I never take that privilege lightly. I refuse to behave like an arrogant, spoiled King's kid, wielding my scepter of power, acting like it's the entitlement of my life. But when I come before Him in grace and emptiness, I get the fullness of the Kingdom.

It's the privilege of my life to get to see what I get to see. I continue to be truly humbled by each miracle that I have the joy of seeing because I truly know and believe that without Him, I can do nothing.

---------------------- ◌ʒ ----------------------

THE POWER OF REMEMBERING

I just returned from the most incredible vacation with my family on a cruise from Seattle, Washington up into Alaska via the inside passage where we got to see the famous Tracy Arm Glacier.

On one of our port stops in Alaska, we took a small bus tour in the hope of seeing a grizzly bear. We asked the driver if there was any chance of seeing a grizzly bear, and he replied, "Well, you never know. Sometimes we do, and sometimes we don't." I went with great expectation that we would, as I know that if it matters to me, it matters to God.

We had stopped at a scenic river, and we were all out of the bus enjoying the scenery, when a car pulled up alongside the driver and told him that there was a grizzly bear around the next bend. The bus driver asked us promptly to get on board. We all loaded into the bus and were given the instructions to be as silent as possible as any noise may scare the bear, and he would take off.

One of my daughters has the habit of making noises at her time of choice without consideration for others. I was thinking she was about to destroy this trip for the other paying guests on this tour, and it would all be our fault. The bus came around the bend, and there in front of us was the amazing sight of a grizzly bear, grazing on the grass, like he had no cares in the world.

The bus had large glass doors on the back as well as the front. The driver pulled right alongside the bear, and it was within six feet of the rear back glass doors. It was amazing. The bus driver whispered and reminded us to be very silent. We all got to the side of the bus and were taking photos, when my daughter screamed.

The bear looked toward us, stared and looked back at the grass and continued to graze on the grass. I was saved! Well, she screamed again and even louder. I felt like the others on the bus were ready to throw us to the bear. The bear looked again, turned toward the bus, approached the bus closer and stood on his back legs in full height. It was simply spectacular.

The cameras were clicking and I have some wonderful photos from three cameras up close with a grizzly bear. I was ready to receive financial tips from the others on the bus.

I also have spectacular footage of approaching the Tracy Arm Glacier from the ship, which was the closest the captain said he has ever got to it in his 26 years of taking this journey as captain.

On the return back to Redding, I was sitting in my pool one hot summer day, and I began to think about our vacation and why we use cameras and take photos and videos.

I was thinking about the memories that are held in a photo or a video. The purpose for the camera is to take a photo, in order to be able to look back and remember the great things of the past and happy memories. All my photos are of the things that I want to remember. I don't have any photos or videos of the things that I do not want to remember.

A key element to the healing ministry is learning to stay encouraged. I have many people say to me, "It must be easy for you to stay encouraged with all the miracles that you see." While I get to see many thousands of miracles each year, it would be just as easy to get discouraged. There are many times that I have failed to see breakthrough and have lost many close people to me. I have had to teach myself to put my focus on what God has done and is doing, not on what has not happened. I must focus on what has happened.

Israel had been delivered from Egypt's bondage by plagues, but they forgot. He rolled back the Red Sea like a scroll, and they passed through on dry ground, but they forgot. He fed them manna and gave them water from a rock, their shoes grew with their feet and their clothes never wore out, but they forgot. They were destroyed in the desert because of their unbelief. *They could not remember who He was or believe what He would do for them.* When the second generation came to the Jordan, He instructed them to never forget what He had done.

In Joshua 4, when the whole nation was finally across, God spoke to Joshua:

> *"Take for yourselves twelve stones from here, out of the midst of the Jordan, from the place where the priests' feet stood firm. You shall carry them over with you and leave them in the lodging place where you lodge tonight."*
>
> *Then Joshua called the twelve men whom he had appointed from the children of Israel, one man from every tribe; and Joshua said to them: "Cross over before the ark of the Lord your God into the midst of the Jordan, and each one of you take up a stone on his shoulder, according to the number of the tribes of the children of Israel, that this may be a sign among you when your children ask in time to come, saying, 'What do these stones mean to you?' Then you shall answer them that the waters of the Jordan were cut off before the ark of the covenant of the Lord; when it crossed over the Jordan, the waters of the Jordan were cut off. And these stones shall be for a memorial to the children of Israel forever"* (Joshua 4:3-7).

Joshua 4:24 gives the reason for the stones. Joshua was saying:

Yes, God, your God, dried up the Jordan's waters for you until you had crossed, just as God, your God, did at the Red Sea, which had dried up before us until we had crossed. This was so that everybody on earth would recognize how strong God's rescuing hand is and so that you would hold God in solemn reverence always (Joshua 4:24 MSG).

It's very easy to forget God's faithfulness.

In Second Timothy, Paul tells Timothy, "I am *reminded* of your sincere faith, which first lived in your grandmother Lois and in your mother Eunice and, I am persuaded, now lives in you also" (2 Tim. 1:5 NIV). God's faithfulness was part of Timothy's family heritage. His grandmother trusted the Lord, and the Lord never failed her or let her down. His mother trusted the Lord, and she was also never failed or let down. Timothy was dealing with great stress and difficulty, and Paul took the opportunity to *remind* him that just as God had never failed his grandmother or his mother, neither would He abandon Timothy.

Then Paul told Timothy in Second Timothy 1:6, "I put thee in *remembrance* that thou stir up the gift of God, which is in thee by the putting on of my hands" (2 Tim. 1:6 KJV). I want you to focus on "I put in remembrance." It is taken from a Greek word *anamimnesko*, a compound word consisting of *ana* and *mimnesko*. The word *ana* means "again" or "repeat something," and the second word, *mimnesko*, means "to be reminded of something such as memories."

When these two words are joined together, it means "to re-gather" or "to recollect memories." The little word, *ana*, carries the idea of replaying these memories over and over again, reminding us of the past times when He has healed us, delivered us, and rescued us over and over. Just like Joshua, we must never forget what God has done for us. Sometimes you just need to remind yourself and never forget how:

- God has healed you.

- God has delivered you.

- God has saved you.

- God has guided and directed you.

- God has brought you through difficult trials.

- God has provided for you during financially trouble-some times.

- God has protected you from the snare of the enemy.

There is incredible power in remembering the miracles and God's faithfulness of the past. We have an amazing 24/7 prayer chapel at Bethel. I love it when I get to take the opportunity to go in there. I enjoy taking communion with the little communion packs there that have inscribed on the top: "This is My body which is given for you, do this in *remembrance of Me*" (Luke 22:19). As I hold the cup and the bread, I always focus my attention on this Scripture and love to remind myself that it's not about me; it's about Jesus. I remind myself of the price that He paid and that the price is paid in full. That it is all about His grace. Even on my very best day, when I feel so full of faith, even that day is still by His amazing grace.

There is something very powerful about reminding yourself of the past miracles and God's faithfulness. The Bible actually mentions "remembering" 64 times. In Matthew 16 and Mark 8, we see the story of when the disciples were out on the boat with Jesus. In Matthew 16:8, we see the disciples had forgotten to take bread, and Jesus said to them, "O you of little faith, why do you reason among yourselves because you have brought no bread?" See, it was only a short time earlier that they had seen the feeding of the 5,000 from just a few fish and seven loaves of bread, and now they were complaining because they were hungry as they had forgotten to take a packed lunch. They saw food produced for 4,000 from almost nothing, and now they couldn't even produce a snack.

Jesus said, "Having eyes, do you not see? And having ears, do you not hear? And do you not remember? When I broke the five loaves for the five thousand, how many baskets full of fragments did you take up?" (Mark 8:18-19). Many times when I go into a healing meeting, I may not always know, understand, hear, or see what God is doing. But there is always one thing that I can do. I can live out of what God has already done and remind myself of that. People say to me, "But I don't see miracles like you have seen," and my answer to them is, "Whoever said that the miracles needed to have been through you?"

There's a great book you can purchase that is full of them; it's called the Bible. See, they are all His miracles, anyway. When we read a testimony of what God has done, we now have a benchmark and a history of what has already happened that we can remember and minister out of. I want to make sure that I am always aligning myself to His track record, as His is pretty impressive.

When I first received this revelation, I did not want to preach about it until I had the practical experience of what I felt like the Lord was showing me.

A few years ago I was in South America, and a young girl came to me and asked me to pray for her back and legs. She had platform shoes on, as one of her legs was about four to five inches shorter than the other. My first reaction was fear. The sole on one foot was up past her ankle on the other. I prayed for a while, and nothing was happening, and the more that I saw nothing happening, the harder my prayer seemed to get, as if I was trying to make something happen.

My daughter, who was eight at the time, was on the other side of the room, so I thought that it would be best to bring some childlike faith into the picture. My daughter joined me, and then I remembered what God had been showing me about the power of remembering what He has done. I said, "But God, I am not sure that I have ever had a leg grow out."

It was so clear as He said, "So you have never seen a leg grow out, at all?" I remembered that just a month or so earlier on a Sunday night, Pastor Bill Johnson had asked if there was anybody who had a leg shorter than the other that was confirmed by a doctor. A lady came forward and sat on a chair that was on the platform. I was watching on a video screen as her leg grew out at least an inch. I began to replay the memory of this miracle over and over in my mind and within a matter of a short time, the girl's knee shook, and I knew that something was in the process of happening.

I shifted the way that I was praying and began to give thanks for what was happening. Right then the leg shot out the entire four to five inches, and the girl screamed so loud, I thought I had hurt her. She leaped out the chair and took me dancing back and forward along the front of the church.

Let me emphasize the point by a couple of other testimonies. One Saturday in the Healing Rooms, I got to pray for two people who were totally deaf in their left ears from birth. No matter what I prayed or how long I prayed, nothing was happening. Wednesday of the next week, I was at a meeting where both of these men were present, and a third person asked me to pray for his deaf ear. With only a short prayer, the man's ear popped open and was fully restored.

I suddenly remembered the power of remembering what God has done, and I took off across the room toward the two men I had prayed for the Saturday before. I approached the first man, told him what had just happened, was lifting my hand toward his ear and within seconds, before my hand even reached his ear, it popped open. I did not hang around long enough to celebrate, as I saw the other man from Saturday, so I took off to also tell him what had just happened. I released the testimony, lifted my hand to pray, and again without my hand even reaching his ear, it popped open.

While ministering out of the country, a man came to me,said that he suffered from Crohn's Disease and asked if I had ever seen that healed. At that point, I had not, but did not want to tell him that. I suddenly remembered another testimony that my father had shared with me of a young girl he was asked to pray for who had Crohn's and was scheduled for a colostomy. He prayed, and the girl was healed.

I shared the testimony with the man and asked how he would know that he was healed. He replied that his stomach area is so sensitive that he couldn't even touch it. I prayed briefly, and he started poking his stomach with amazement in his face. I asked if there was another way that he could test it. He said, "I could not do one sit-up."

I said, "Why don't you try one while I pray for these other people?"

He was gone for a few minutes, came back and tapped me on the shoulder and said, "I just did 40 sit-ups."

I returned to the USA, and within a few weeks, I was in another healing conference, where I was sharing this story. A man stood up in the middle of my message and shouted out, "I have Crohn's."

"The testimony of Jesus is the spirit of prophecy" (Rev. 19:10). When we testify of what God has done, we are making a prophetic declaration of what is going to happen. We create an atmosphere for the miracle to be duplicated. As the man stood, I pointed at him and said, "The testimony of Jesus is the spirit of prophecy." I saw the miracle come out of my mouth, fly across the room and hit him right in the stomach. He fell into his chair, and I carried on preaching. I wanted to talk to him as I knew something significant had happened, but he left immediately after the service.

The following morning, he came to the meeting and introduced himself to me as the man who had Crohn's. I asked him how he would know if he were healed and why he left immediately after the service. He replied that because of the disease he couldn't eat any junk food or dairy products. But because he knew he was healed, he left to go and get a triple cheeseburger. He felt so good that he went back to get a milk shake for breakfast.

Several weeks later, he e-mailed to say that he had been to the doctor and had an endoscopy, and there was no trace of Crohn's found, and the doctor has taken him off medication.

I have seen the miracle of Crohn's duplicated a number of times simply by sharing about the power of the testimony and living out of my history with God, by stewarding and remembering what He has done.

MINISTERING OUT OF ABUNDANCE

I must learn to minister out of my history of what I have seen God do, what He is doing, and His track record. Yet many people live out of their own track record, and they wonder why they fail to see breakthrough in their lives. Let's say that you are ministering to a person who has Crohn's, yet you have never seen someone healed of Crohn's through you. Many would minister and think about the last person they never got healed or worse, the last one who actually died. When we do that, we are ministering out of our track record, and that's great if we see 100 percent of those who come to us get healed. But instead of doing that, choose to align yourself to His track record; 100 percent of those who came to Him were healed. Next time you get to minister to someone, think about the last time you have seen or heard about that miracle happening. When we minister out of remembering what we have seen, we are ministering out of His abundance, but when we minister out of remembering what we have not seen, we are ministering out of lack. We must do everything that we can to stay in faith/abundance, and the best way that this can be done is by remembering what Jesus has done and is doing.

Once you have seen or heard a miracle of what Jesus has done, it changes the way that you minister. You can never pray from lack again for any condition that you have read or heard about. When I do conferences, I often release words of knowledge simply out of my history or what I have seen God do, and I get to see the same miracles duplicated over and over again. If you have never seen a miracle, then take the miracles in this book, or better still, read the Bible; it's full of them. Next time you get to pray for someone with Crohn's or any condition, remember these miracles or the miracles in your Bible, and minister from the abundance of faith.

Stewarding the testimony is so important for the reasons above. I have thousands of testimonies on my computer, and at conferences I ask people to send them to me. The importance of stewarding the testimony of what God has done is a critical part of growing in the supernatural. Not only are they important for us; God, Himself, loves them.

> *Your testimonies I have taken as a heritage forever, for they are the rejoicing of my heart* (Psalms 119:111).

God rejoices over each testimony. It's important that we share testimonies of what God has done. I often say in healing conferences that if we are not prepared to share the testimony, which gives God the glory, then we are actually taking His glory.

─────────────── ○ ───────────────

CHAPTER 11

ARE THERE ROADBLOCKS TO HEALING?

One of the largest obstacles to healing is not the lack of faith as I have already written about, but the presence of doubts. When we learn to recognize that the answer to every situation that we face is larger than the problem that is in front of us, then the obstacles become less of an issue. Yet many people have created their theologies around the presence of obstacles to help justify their lack of power and breakthrough.

It can be very easy to project onto the person we are ministering to and make the obstacle larger than it actually is simply by bringing their attention to it.

Personally, my main focus is to not bring the person's attention to what they think the problem is, or might be, but to get their eyes onto the answer, Jesus Christ.

How many articles or books have you read that go into great detail as to why people are not healed? This is not my personal approach. I just want to be so consumed with the answer, that no roadblock or obstacle would be able to stand in the way.

I love to tell people that if they want a ministry like Jesus had, then they should just do what Jesus did. In reading the accounts of Jesus through

Scripture, I don't see where He addressed the problem. He just released the answer because the atmosphere that He carried was greater than the problem of those coming to Him. There was an occasion in Mark 10:51 when Jesus asked blind Bartimaeus, "What do you want Me to do for you?"

One would think that it's pretty obvious. Blind Bartimaeus was blind; that's why his name was "blind Bartimaeus." So why did Jesus ask him the question? Jesus had His atmosphere, and the man had his own atmosphere. Maybe Jesus was testing him to see if sickness had become his identity. Maybe the man did not even want healing; maybe he wanted a simple blessing or maybe Jesus wanted him to vocalize what he wanted to initiate faith.

There are occasions when people simply do not want to be healed as sickness has become their identity. When this is the case, I still need to love them. In the case of blind Bartimaeus, He did not just release the answer. He asked first, "What do you want Me to do for you?"

In John 9:2-3, we see the story of the man that was born blind from birth. Jesus' disciples asked Him, "Rabbi, who sinned, this man or his parents, that he was born blind?" Jesus answered, "Neither this man nor his parents sinned, but that the works of God should be revealed in him."

God is bigger than our roadblocks. I am sure that the man and his parents would have sinned some time in life. Yet we see that Jesus was more interested in the works of God being revealed. If we need to be perfect to be healed, then we are coming on our own merits for healing and very few of us would be healed or would qualify to be used by God.

I hope that this would not need to be said, but I know that I will be taken out of context and be quoted as saying that I am promoting a license to sin. That is simply not the truth or my heart. People who choose to willfully sin are not really looking for a license to sin; they will sin anyway, and that's just the spirit of stupid. I want to see people healed in all dimensions of their lives walking in the freedom that Christ purchased body, soul, and spirit.

People come with their obstacles as to why they think they should not be healed. I do believe that they can come with their obstacles, which could potentially block their healing. However, I choose to believe that if I carry the answer in such a manner in my life that the answer is bigger than the problem, then their obstacle does not need to become my obstacle.

Let me give you an example. Let's say someone comes to you for a miracle. We pray, and it appears that nothing has happened. So in our powerlessness, we ask them if there is any un-forgiveness in their life. What have we just done? We have projected our powerlessness onto them in the absence of a miracle. I have now got them to take their eyes off the answer and have had them look inside. They are now looking at the problem and their shortfalls, and it is pretty hard to look inside and come out feeling great.

When you begin to see miracles in your life, and especially when you are more known for walking in power, then the person you are ministering to thinks that you hear from God extremely clearly, and He is whispering all the dirt about them into your ear. We don't need anyone to tell us our dirt; we already know our own.

This is where I am taken out of context: that I only care about the physical healing and do not care if they have sin or un-forgiveness in their lives. That is simply not true. If, while ministering to a person, I feel the Lord say to me that there is un-forgiveness that needs to be dealt with or drops a name into my heart (for example, their father), then I still don't ask directly if they have any un-forgiveness toward their father. I would in casual conversation begin to ask them about their life and the town they live in, and where they were raised. I ask the right questions, and most times, they end up telling me the problem without me projecting a problem that might or might not be there. What if I had not heard the Lord correctly? Now they think I have seen a problem of un-forgiveness, and they are introspective, soul-searching, looking for the dirt I just highlighted.

But when I ask the questions out of relationship and a genuine heart for the person, they nearly always end up telling me the answers that I need to hear, and then I can assist in bringing freedom to that person.

A person came to me in an evening healing meeting and asked me to pray for her heroin addiction. "Of course I will." I asked her what her name was. I immediately heard what I thought was the Lord speaking to me that there was an un-forgiveness issue toward her mother.

I asked her, "Were you raised in this city? Have you always lived here? Do your parents still live here?"

To that she replied, "No, they are in hell burning, and it's a good place for them."

Well, then I knew there was a problem and I was hearing from God correctly. I asked her if I could ask a question and said that she would need to work with me on the answer. I asked, "Let's just say that your mother is in Heaven."

She laughed and said, "I can't work with that. My mother abused me all my life. Sorry Chris, but she's in hell."

I replied, "That's why I need you to work with me. Let's just say she is in heaven."

She now said, "OK. I'm working with you now."

"So would she be having a good life or a bad life?" I asked.

"She would be having an amazing time with Jesus."

"Exactly," I replied. "So now answer me this. Who is the one left in this relationship having a bad experience in life?"

"That would be me," she replied.

"So do you want to do something about that?"

"Yes, please. I'm miserable, Chris."

I was then able to lead her through a forgiveness prayer, and that night she was wonderfully set free from the addiction of drugs by the power of Jesus.

While I thought that I had clearly heard God about the issue, I still never projected the problem onto her by telling her what the problem was.

I simply asked the right questions and she told me everything that I needed to know, so that I could quickly deal with the issue and see freedom come.

What if you were getting prayer regularly for the same issue over and over again and all that you were ever told to justify the lack of power from the person or persons ministering was, "Do you have un-forgiveness?" or their prayer was always rebuking a spirit or coming against the problem, yet you still were not healed? You would really begin to think that you had a pretty big devil that could not be shifted.

It's the same with root causes. If the person is not getting healed, I won't default to projecting my lack of power upon them by suggesting that there is a root cause. Addressing these kinds of issues without wisdom tends to lead to introspection.

There may be times when a direct confrontation about an issue is necessary, and I am not saying that this never happens. I am just saying that I do this with extreme caution and not just because I did not see someone healed when I prayed. I would rather go on my face before God and pray that I get a greater revelation of who He is in me and through me, and gain a greater understanding of the revelation of His goodness and the power of His love.

I am more interested in learning to release life and living out of the abundance of the answer that lives in me, because there is no problem that I will ever encounter that is bigger than the answer. There is no sickness or disease in life that has not been paid for in full by the blood of Jesus!

CHAPTER 12

───────────── ঞ ─────────────

THE POWER OF IMPARTATION

I feel the best way to write about the power of impartation is to write from a personal perspective of what I have come through to walk in a life of power. I estimate that I prayed for in excess of 1,000 people before I saw any breakthrough. I had become frustrated in ministry from not seeing any results. There was nobody around me who was walking in a lifestyle of miracles. I had heard a lot of teaching, but had seen very limited demonstration. The best thing that I felt I could do was to get near as many people as possible who were walking in a daily life of miracles.

The first place of call was to attend a healing school with Randy Clark in Pennsylvania. On the way from New Zealand to Randy's healing school, I stopped for a weekend at Bethel Church in Redding, California, where I had most of my paradigms shifted through their teaching. The impartation that came from the teaching of the Word was amazing and literally shifted my mindset and what and how I was teaching.

From Bethel, I went on to Randy Clark's healing school. One night he was teaching, and it was an impartation night, when he was going to pray for everyone who wanted prayer from him. Before the altar call was given, it was like a magnet had pulled me right out of my seat, and I found myself at the front of the church before anyone else had even stood. I was that hungry to receive prayer. I looked behind me to see that I had about 1,000 others following. I remember this so clearly, as Randy laid his hand on my head and prayed, and I felt like I had been electrocuted directly from Heaven. I can remember flying through the air and hitting the floor and shaking violently for well over an hour. I finally crawled on my hands and knees back to my chair, where I was sitting next to one of Randy's interns. They looked at me and laughed and said, "What happened to you?" I tried to explain what had happened, and they laid their hand on my head and said, "More God." On that, I flipped over the back of the chair and found myself under my chair for the rest of the evening, as God was doing something very deep in my heart. I knew that something had changed, and I knew that an adventure was ahead for me.

On the flight back to New Zealand a couple of days later, I was in the Chicago airport enjoying a deep pan pizza and was simply thinking about what had happened. On that, I fell face first into my pizza, overwhelmed by the presence of God. As I sat up, I had a string of cheese hanging from my face and shirt.

Today I continue to take as many opportunities as I can to receive prayer from anybody who walks in a greater level of miracles than I do, and I have had some incredible opportunities to receive prayer from many of the world's greatest revivalists. I do what I can to be around great men and women of God, to serve and ask questions.

Today as I get to host healing schools and conferences around the world, I have many people asking for impartation from me, and I love to take opportunities to have impartation services. Several years after I started walking in miracles, the Lord began to intensify to me the revelation of "Christ in you, the hope of glory." I began to realize that many people come and ask for impartation out of a place of desperation as they think they have nothing. However, the Bible says in First John 2:20 that we already have an anointing from the Holy One.

My perspective on impartation is that we as believers already have the original flame of Pentecost burning on our heads, so it's not the impartation that necessarily lights the flame, but I see it as putting gasoline on the fire that we as believers already each carry. We each have a flame, but our flames are all different sizes depending on how we have stewarded our walk with the Lord.

I totally believe in impartation and the transference that is possible when we come to honor the gift that is on another person. However, also just as important is how we steward what we have received.

I tell people all the time that I can pray for them, and there will be some who fall to the ground and have a similar experience to what I had when Randy prayed for me. However, I have seen people who have had such an experience, yet did nothing with what they received and nothing actually changed in their lives. Similarly, I have seen people I have prayed for who have felt nothing, but because we receive by faith and not by feeling, these people walked from the meetings, believed that they received something, began to give away what they received, and began to see incredible miracles through their hands.

I had never seen a miracle through my hands until I had Randy Clark and Bill Johnson pray for me within the same few days. The very next day, I saw the very first miracle through me. I understood that what I had received needed to be stewarded, for the impartation is only as good as what we choose to do with it.

I intentionally went out of my way to pray for people from that day. I have to put myself in a position of risk, having believed that I received gasoline on the fire that burns within me. I have seen miracles weekly from that very day, and as I have learned to steward what I have seen, I have only seen increase in my life. As I continue to give thanks for even the small, I have been blessed to see some of the most amazing miracles that I once could only dream about.

Many people go from impartation to impartation, yet fail to do anything with what they receive. To increase in what we receive it's so important that we learn to give it away.

Give, and it will be given to you: good measure, pressed down, shaken together, and running over... (Luke 6:38).

I so love and believe in the power of impartation, yet there must come a point that we actually believe that we carry the very present reality of the Holy Spirit. If we don't believe that we have the hope of glory living inside us, then how will we ever give Him away, when we are not in a position of having someone to pray impartation prayers over us?

I am the first to continue to receive prayer from anyone who walks in a greater level of miracles than what I have got to see, but I do not approach impartation from a perspective that I do not have anything, that I do not have the original flame of Pentecost burning on my head. I approach it from the perspective that I have the original flame, and I want some gasoline thrown on my fire.

Throughout the Bible are examples regarding impartation and the importance of the laying on of hands.

In Matthew 19:13-15, we see the little children were brought to Jesus so that He could lay hands on them. This passage does not directly reference that they were brought to Jesus for healing, even though we know that He healed people wherever He went. Jesus said, "Let the little children come to Me, and do not be forbid them; for of such is the kingdom of heaven" (Matt. 19:14).

In Mark 16:18, we see Jesus, Himself, pronouncing the great commission, "...They will lay hands on the sick, and they will recover." There is impartation that takes place in the laying on of hands for healing. In Acts 13:1-3, we see the laying on of hands for the commissioning or ordaining In Matthew 19:13-15, we see the little children were brought to Jesus so that He could lay hands on them. This passage does not directly reference that they were brought to Jesus for healing, even though we know that He healed people wherever He went. Jesus said, "Let the little children come to Me, and do not be forbid them; for of such is the kingdom of heaven" (Matt. 19:14).

missionaries. Barnabas and Saul were brought and had hands laid on them; then they were sent away, sent out by the Holy Spirit.

In Acts 19:11-12, we see the anointing must be tangible and transferable. "Now God worked unusual miracles by the hands of Paul, so that even handkerchiefs or aprons were brought from his body to the sick, and diseases left them and the evil spirits went out of them."

In First Timothy 4:14, we see the laying on of hands for the ordination. "Do not neglect the gift that is in you, which was given to you by prophecy with the laying on of the hands of the eldership."

In Romans 1:11-12, we can see the concept for impartation. "I long to see you, that I may impart to you some spiritual gift, so that you may be established—that is, that I may be encouraged together with you by the mutual faith both of you and me."

I think that we have often limited impartation to purely the laying on of hands. I have seen many people disappointed because they were not able to have hands laid on them at a conference. They then think that they have not received an impartation because of this.

However, we can receive a powerful impartation by sitting under the teaching/preaching of the Word. Some of the most powerful impartations that I have personally received have been sitting under the teaching of the Word.

Like I already stressed, I do not fully understand how impartation works; however, I will continue to get the laying on of hands and sit under the Word from people who walk in a greater level of the miraculous than I have yet had the joy of seeing.

I have gone out of my way, even at incredible inconvenience, to have many great men and women of God pray for me. I had the joy of getting to spend time over a meal with Mrs. Freda Lindsay (Gordon Lindsay's wife, founder of Christ for the Nations) just a few months before she went to be with the Lord. I was able to honor Mrs. Lindsay for the price that they both paid for the gospel over the past number of decades. I have always seen increase in fruitfulness as I have placed myself in the position of humility in asking these amazing people to pray over my life and give advice for keys in partnering with Heaven, increasing in the anointing, and deepening my relationship with God, while never neglecting or denying the understanding and revelation of the Spirit of the risen Christ that is already with me. Mrs. Freda Lindsay's advice was to always walk in humility about what God does through you. I love impartation and the increase that I have always experienced when others have prayed for me, while not despising the one that already lives within me

CHAPTER 13

FRIENDSHIP WITH JESUS

This would have to be one of the most important chapters if not *the* most important chapter that I have written. The foundation for walking in a life of miracles is the understanding that it is not just us in Him, but it is Him in us. That is our identity; our identity is in Him and in Him alone. It is not in what I do, but it is in what He has done.

But there is a greater underlying truth to our identity, and that would have to be our friendship with Jesus. How can we develop true identity outside of friendship with God, Himself? Would our identity then only become one of head knowledge? There is nothing wrong with principles, but one of the greatest dangers in writing on walking in the supernatural would be that anyone could take the principles of walking in miracles and just apply the principles to their lives without friendship with the Prince, Himself, and still see a level of fruitfulness of miracles through their lives.

We could be seeing miracles through our lives and be fully dependent upon His grace and friendship. Then when we begin to see a more constant flow of the miraculous, we actually think that we are doing OK because we are seeing fruit and come to the conclusion that we really have become so good at our job that we can do it independent of friendship with God and His grace.

I was out driving one day with Emma, my middle daughter, and out of the blue she asked me a question. She said, "Dad, if there was one thing in the entire world that you could have, what would it be?" Before I had the opportunity to answer, she said, "Don't answer. I already know what it is. You would want Charlotte to be healed."

Without even thinking about the answer to that statement, my answer rolled off my mouth, and I said, "No, Emma, there is something that I want more than that. I would want greater friendship with God and to be able to hear His voice with even greater clarity." I continued, "If I could hear His voice with greater clarity, then I would see the fruitfulness of seeing Charlotte healed."

She thought for a minute, and then said, "But Dad, I know that you love to see miracles and see the sick healed, so what if you could see the entire world healed of disease?"

Without hesitation, I replied, "No, Emma, it would still be to have a greater relationship with God and a greater clarity of His voice."

Please don't get me wrong on this. I don't have to choose one over the other. I get to enjoy both, but if it was the choice of only one, it would be relationship with God, Himself. I know that He lives in me and that He is not out there apart from me, but my quest in life is to know Him more. The greatest joy of my life is to just know Him and to be known by Him. To take the time to be friends with the King of all kings, to take time in worshiping at His feet and taking time to be in His Word, not to see more miracles, even though I want this, but it's just to know Him. One of the greatest joys is to study the Word of God, and as Pastor Bill Johnson has clearly stated, "I don't study to preach. I study for my sake." I study the Word and spend time with Him because I want to know Him and understand more of His love and nature that He has toward me. The overflow of my relationship that I have with God is what the people around me get to enjoy. The overflow of my relationship with God is the flow of the supernatural as I become immersed in His nature.

One of my favorite Old Testament books is the book of Ruth. It is an amazing romance story of what happened between Ruth and Boaz. There is some incredible revelation of Jesus in the book of Ruth. Jesus is there in the person of Boaz. Boaz was a wealthy man of Bethlehem. Jesus is seen throughout the Old Testament and represented though the life of several Old Testament people.

Let's first look at some of the history of the story of Ruth. The story of Ruth was set in 1322 BC. The very name of Ruth means "beauty" and "a friend." Ruth was not a Jew; she was a Moabite. Ruth's great-grandson was David, and David's son was Solomon. We know that Solomon was the richest and wealthiest king known on earth. We are told that Ruth's mother-in-law was Naomi. Naomi left Israel, known as the land of promise, and fled to Moab, known as an idolatrous land. When Naomi left the land of promise, she took her husband and her two sons with her. One of her sons married Ruth, and the other son married a lady called Orpah.

The names of the sons of Naomi were Mahlon (which means "sickness") and Chilion (which means "wasting away"). We are told that both the husband of Naomi and her two sons died. (Little surprise with names like that!)

With their passing away, both Mahlon and Chilion left behind widows, Ruth and Orpah (which means "stiff-necked" or "double-minded"). After their husbands passed away, Orpah decided stay in Moab, and Ruth decided to follow Naomi, her mother-in-law, back to Bethlehem (which means "house of bread"). Naomi had heard that God was blessing the people in Bethlehem.

Naomi is an incredible picture of Israel, and Ruth is a picture of you and me because we are not Jews (well I am not), yet we still get everything that God promised Abraham. Why? Because the seed of Abraham is our Lord Jesus Christ. Jesus took us as His bride. It does not matter what you do;

when a prince marries you, you are no longer a low- to middle-class person; you become a princess. (Guys, you just need to get over this one.) You now take his name, and all that the prince possesses becomes yours.

Now let's look at the person of Boaz. He was a man of great wealth. (His name means "strength.") So we have Naomi and Ruth who have gone back to the land of promise, and we see in Ruth chapter 2 that Ruth asks Naomi to let her go to the field and glean heads of grain after him in whose sight she may find favor. And she happened to come to the part of the field that belonged to Boaz. Ruth comes back from Boaz with a blessing. She comes back with an ephah of barley, which is a Jewish measurement of a ten-day supply.

> *And her mother-in-law said to her, "Where have you gleaned today? And where did you work? Blessed be the one who took notice of you."*
>
> *So she told her mother-in-law with whom she had worked, and said, "The man's name with whom I worked today is Boaz"* (Ruth 2:19).

Ruth mentions to Naomi the name of Boaz, and Naomi says, "This man is a relation of ours, one of our close relatives" (Ruth 2:20). When Naomi and Ruth came back from Moab, they came back poor.

A provision in the law of Moses allows that if someone forfeits their land because of poverty or moving away, a close relative can buy it back for them. It's called kinsman redeemer or relative redeemer. Now Naomi had forfeited her family's land by her absence of ten years.

Christ Jesus is known as our redeemer. Even if we have lost our health, even when it's due to our own fault because of neglect, our redeemer Christ Jesus can buy back for us what we have lost. That's why He is called "redeemer." He can buy back and redeem.

Jesus is represented by this person called Boaz, and He's a kinsman redeemer. So for a redeemer to first buy back your land, there are three requirements that he must first fulfill:

1. He must be a relative. (That's why God came in human flesh, to be our relative, to be part of the human race. To be our redeemer, He had to be part of the human race to redeem man.)

2. He must be willing. Is Jesus willing? Yes, on the cross, we saw Him with outstretched hands. He bought us back, out of the slave market of sin, poverty, and the curse. He is truly our redeemer.

3. He must be wealthy. We know from this story that Boaz is wealthy. Sound like someone else we know? The one who owns the cattle on a thousand hills? Yes. Jesus Christ.

Ruth now knows that Boaz is one of the close relatives. Jesus does not want to be one of our helpers, or one of our redeemers. He wants to be *the* redeemer. He is the one and only true redeemer.

Naomi tells Ruth, "Tonight Boaz is threshing barley on the threshing floor" (see Ruth 3:2). The threshing floor was normally in an elevated place and they would thresh the barley at night because the winds were always stronger. They would thresh the bundles of barley and then take a pitchfork and take the barley and throw it into the air. The barley is heavier and the shaft is lighter, so when they throw it in the air, the shaft is blown away, and what falls down is barley.

So Boaz was doing this at night with some of his men, and Naomi said to Ruth, "Bathe, put on nice clothes and anoint yourself with perfume and go to where Boaz is" (see Ruth 3:3). This was the custom of the day. Ruth would propose to Boaz.

We must not forget that Boaz is an amazing picture of our Lord Jesus Christ. The book of Ruth is full of wonderful pictures of our heavenly Boaz, Jesus Christ. So what happened when she fell at his feet? Being at Jesus' feet, you make Him so incredibly big. It's an act of worship and humility. Whenever we read in the Gospels that some came to Jesus' feet, they received their miracle.

They received His redeeming power. If they had a disease, the disease had to go. There is something very powerful about coming to the feet of Jesus in an act of worship and humility. Every time we come to His feet, we receive from Him.

There are several accounts of people coming to the feet of Jesus! We read in Mark 5:22 that Jairus was a ruler of the synagogue whose 12-year-old daughter was dying. The daughter died, but Jairus fell at Jesus' feet, and his daughter was raised from the dead.

Here's another example:

> *Now it happened as they went that He entered a certain village; and a certain woman named Martha welcomed Him into her house. And she had a sister called Mary, who also sat at Jesus feet and heard His word* (Luke 10:38-39).

And another:

> *And one of them, when he saw he was healed, returned, and with a loud voice glorified God, and fell down on his face at His feet, giving Him thanks...and He said to him, "Arise, go your way. Your faith has made you well"* (Luke 17:15-16,19).

In Mark 7:25, we find that the Syro-Phoenician woman's daughter had an unclean spirit, and she came and fell at His feet. As a result, Jesus cast the devil out from a distance, and she went home and her daughter was set free.

When we come to worship Jesus, we are all at His feet; we are all on the same ground, and Jesus is exalted and lifted up.

Boaz awakes, and he says:

> *Now it is true that I am a close relative; however, there is a relative closer than I. Stay this night, and in the morning it shall be that if he will perform the duty of a close relative for you—good;*

let him do it. But if he does not want to perform the duty for you, then I will perform the duty for you, as the Lord lives! Lie down until morning (Ruth 3:12-13).

I feel that the one message that the Lord has been speaking to me most about over the years is to make sure we are taking the time to lie down and rest at His feet. We can get so busy working and doing things for God that we can forget where the actual source comes from. The very source of what we have the incredible privilege to take part in around the world today is taking time to be at the feet of Jesus!

I long to see a generation of revivalists moving strongly in the supernatural but not merely preoccupied with it. I long to see a generation of revivalists so smitten with Jesus that the miraculous is simply the byproduct. The last thing I want to see is a people who know how to do miracles, but don't know the miracle maker Himself. I want to see people grow in their relationship and love with the creator, Himself, and people who become solid in God's Word.

One day, a number of years back, the Lord spoke to me so loudly: "You love what you do for Me more than you love Me."

I am an extremely task-orientated person. I find it super hard to sit still and be still for even five minutes, but I have to take time to sit at His feet and take time in worship and feed on Jesus and His Word. Not for what He can do, but just because of who He is.

It's really easy to fall into the presumption that since you saw a miracle yesterday through you, you must have a great relationship with God.

See, we can know the principles of walking in the supernatural, yet not really know the prince, Himself. My priority has to be knowing God and being known by God. Sometimes this line of thinking is prevalent in a church of the supernatural.

I am not only talking about taking time to enjoy sitting at His feet in worship, but also to physically rest. Taking time out to enjoy His creation, enjoy our families, enjoy leisure, and enjoy a bit of golf. But it's also leading a lifestyle of rest. Miracles come out of rest. Resting in knowing who we are. It's who we are that defines us, not what we do. If we allow what we do to define who we are, then we are heading for trouble. Miracles are not done for identity; they are because of our identity.

Boaz asks:

> "Who are you?" So she answered, "I am Ruth, your maidservant. Take your maidservant under your wing, for you are a close relative" (Ruth 3:9).

When you are a kinsman redeemer and your brother (or relative) dies, you are required to take his wife and marry her to bring up seed for your brother. Boaz goes to the close relative, redeems that land for Naomi, and takes Ruth as his wife. They bear a son called Obed (which means "servant of God, worshiper, and follower").

This is a wonderful story of the friendship between Ruth and Boaz, which represents the same relationship between our redeemer and us. When we take time to come to the feet of our redeemer and take time in worship just because of who He is, when we come empty in the place of humility, acknowledging the greatness of our King, we get the fullness of the King and His Kingdom. He redeems us, restores us, and takes us as His bride. The baseline for walking in miracles must be out of friendship with the King, taking time to worship Him, not because of what He can do but for who He is.

CHAPTER 14

⌘

PRISONER OF HOPE

Come back to the place of safety, all you prisoners who still have hope! I promise this very day that I will repay two blessings for each of your troubles (Zechariah 9:12 NLT).

I wanted to write this chapter to bring hope to anybody who has special-needs children. In fact, it's really to anyone who also has suffered with a long-term condition. My heart burns to see childhood diseases and childhood conditions end. I have gone after the healing of cerebral palsy, autism, Down's, and childhood disabilities for over 17 years. In the past two years, I have started to see some results. When you push on something that seems unmovable, you for sure get stronger. I have seen a dramatic breakthrough with one girl with cerebral palsy and have seen two children healed now of autism. I'm so thankful, but I must see more.

I know what it feels like to be without hope while caring for a special-needs child. I know how easy it is to feel isolated and forgotten by others around you, who find it easier in many cases to turn a blind eye to the cry of help. I must keep my eyes on Jesus. I don't have all the answers, but I know that in the end, it will all work out.

My wife, Liz, is the most incredible wife and mother I know. As we have both walked through our own journey of dealing with a special-needs child, Liz is the one who has had the main share of the childcare and at times it is 24/7 when I get to go away and speak around the world.

I wanted to share this one last testimony in the prayer that it will release incredible hope into your situation, for anyone who has special-needs children or for that matter any sickness at all, especially where the doctors say, "incurable."

We must keep our eye on the prize: the person of Jesus Christ. I know whenever I am feeling discouraged and feeling like hope is lost, it's because I have taken my eye off the truth and focused too long on the facts. I have shifted my focus to what has not happened, as opposed to feeding myself on what Jesus has done.

The following miracle took place in March 2012 and the writing of this chapter took place in March 2013. Hope's story is amazing, and I continue to get regular updates on the breakthroughs that Hope and her parents are seeing. May the testimony of the miracle of this ten-year-old girl named Hope, bring so much hope into your situation and life that you won't be able to help but be a carrier and releaser of hope to all those who are around you. May you receive double for your trouble.

> September 8, 2001, Hope is born! At the age of five, Hope was diagnosed with Asperger's, a form of autism. From that day on, we prayed, talked to doctors, met with therapists, read books, and did everything we could to learn about helping children with autism, but saw very limited progress for Hope.
>
> Everything changed at the healing conference in Kentucky in the spring of 2012 where Chris Gore was ministering. Hope at that time was 10 years old. Chris prayed for Hope as I stood in on her behalf. He simply put his hand on my head and said, "I release the shalom of Heaven." In that moment, I felt liquid peace being poured into my body. I could feel muscles releasing

down my back as the peace poured in. I went back to Hope and simply prayed exactly what Chris prayed. I placed my hand on her head and said," I release the shalom of Heaven." Then she looked at me and said, "Can we go to McDonald's for lunch now?"

Later that night at the conference I saw clouds above me in the spirit. Big white hands came out of the clouds. I could see them operating on my brain, only I knew it was Hope's brain. When I got home, I went into the children's rooms as they were sleeping and laid hands on their heads, praying, "Lord, release all that you did at the conference to them," and I called forth the fullness of their destiny. When I did that for Hope, there was a wind in the spirit that entered the room.

The next morning on the car ride back to the conference, we immediately noticed that Hope just reeked, I mean really, really reeked of fish. When we checked in at the conference, the woman at the registration desk said, "Oh, it smells like someone packed a fish sandwich for lunch!" Hope continued to reek of fish for several weeks. When I asked the Lord what the fish smell was about, I heard in my spirit, "I am detoxifying Hope."

Since the healing, we have seen remarkable changes. At school Hope has been mainstreamed for the first time in her life with no aide, therapist or accommodations at school assigned to her. She is now getting A's and B's!

Socially, she's completely blossomed.

She has had successful overnight sleepovers for the first time in her life. Her friends are asking if they can come over, stay longer, and come back soon! She has become capable of watching her little three-year-old brother and is so patient and sweet with helping him do things. She plans and leads the neighbor children in making crafts. She interacts on a very complex and normal level with people of all ages, including her peers and adults.

We used to give her a ton of vitamin supplements, now her body is rejecting them as if she doesn't need them any more.

Recently, I asked our babysitter if she had noticed that one of our children had developmental difficulties. I asked her which one she thought it was that had the issues. She guessed the wrong child.

Even Hope is noticing the healing changes. "Mom," she said, "I used to be really afraid of the sound of the rain and thunder. Now I'm not! I'm thinking that the drought is probably close to over with all of this rain. I still don't really like the flash of the lightning, but it's over pretty fast." She was grinning ear to ear, and her eyes almost sparkled with the joy of noticing her own healing! We opened the door and watched the rain pouring and the lightning flashing out the front door, side by side, arms around one another for a few very special moments together.

The old diagnosis of Asperger's is no longer relevant. She no longer does the things that define Asperger's Syndrome. She has become engaged, aware of herself and others, witty and full of joy. It's like what had always been there has become unlocked. The life she was meant to live and the person God made her to be are emerging. God is healing Hope!

———————————— ❧ ————————————

CHAPTER 15

FREQUENTLY ASKED QUESTIONS

I wanted to include a chapter on frequently asked questions, as I get the same questions at almost every conference that I attend.

I prayed for someone and nothing happened. Why were they not healed?

This has to be the most commonly asked question that I receive. First off, one of my core values is that it's impossible to pray and have nothing happen. I live with that conviction. I have an obligation to love; they are a person, not a project. If I can love them, they had an encounter with Jesus. Second, I have had hundreds of reports of me praying for someone, and it appears that nothing has happened. But I get the reports days, weeks, or even in some cases, several years later and find out that the miracle happened after they, in fact, left. But the person praying for them may never know the result of the effort of their prayer. I just had a report this week of a young girl who was dramatically healed when I ministered to her over nine months ago. I had no idea this had happened until nine months later.

Another side of this question is about when we know for sure that they are not healed. Why is that?

I pray for a fair share of people whom I have not seen breakthrough for. It would be very easy to create my own theology in the absence of a miracle. We then end up bringing the gospel to our level of experience, as opposed to bringing our experience to the level of the gospel.[1] I do not know why all I pray for are not healed, but I do know that it's God's will and heart to heal all. Jesus healed all who came to Him with no exception. I also refuse to push it under the carpet of God's sovereignty. There is mystery in the healing ministry, but I do not let that stop me from going after all that Jesus paid for.

I will never condemn the person for not being healed. I will not blame God, as He does not sit there and make decisions about who He will heal and who He won't. That decision was made and paid for over 2,000 years ago. There is only one other person in the equation, and that is me, yet I refuse to beat myself up for the lack of the result. When I see someone healed, that is fuel on my fire, and in the same way, when I see someone not healed, that is also fuel on my fire and makes me go after that condition all the more.

I'm seeing breakthrough in my life, but I want to see more. How do I see more healing through my life?

This is a multi-part answer. While not an extensive list, I have listed a few key points. I have seen many people who see a measure of breakthrough, and they want more like we all want to see. However, they don't live out of thanksgiving for what they have seen. They want to see limbs grow back, but they can't even be thankful because a little old lady's headache got healed.

We cannot despise the day of small beginnings; we must live in a place of absolute thankfulness. Even when we are seeing the more dramatic miracles, we need to stay in awe over even the small ones as well as the big ones. Some of the miracles that stick with me the strongest are the small miracles, and I am eternally thankful, because whether it's a big miracle or a small miracle, I can't do either of them. It was all about His grace in me and through me. Without Him, I can do nothing.

Secondly, I position myself to get around anyone who sees greater miracles than I do, to learn, to ask questions, to just be in their atmosphere. That is why I offered to drive Bethel speakers around, so I can just be in the car with them. I have flown to several places to have the opportunity to sit and talk and learn. I have learned some incredible things from taking the time and expense to invest into these opportunities.

Thirdly, see if you can go on ministry trips with these people. In 2006, I went with Randy Clark to India, and a new high-water mark in my life was set. I have also taken others with me on my trips.

Fourthly, the greater revelation I receive of His love, His character, and His nature, and the more that I feed myself on His goodness, the more that faith simply becomes a byproduct and I see more breakthrough. I addressed this more in the chapter on friendship with Jesus.

Fifthly, lead a life of humility. Stay low and stay a novice. There is still so much that I need to learn. Stay a student and never act like you know it all, or have arrived.

I prayed for someone and they were amazingly healed, but within a short period of time, they lost their healing. Why?

First let me say this. God is the healer; He is not the un-healer. We don't see Him heal one day and then the next day remove what He just did. Jesus comes to give life and give it abundantly, and the enemy is the one who comes to kill, steal, and destroy. (See John 10:10.) The enemy wants to do everything that he can to steal from you.

With healing comes responsibility, and sometimes those who have been healed don't take responsibility and steward what they have received. A great example of this would be that I could see you healed from diabetes diabetes, which had developed from a bad lifestyle and being overweight.

You are healed by the power of God, but now comes our part of stewardship. Being healed of diabetes is not permission to indulge in a lifestyle of eating junk. I have seen this happen a few times, and it is rather heartbreaking. I'm an advocate for stewardship of our bodies and treating them well.

I have also seen people who are so works orientated that they do not understand the grace of God. One person whom I saw dramatically healed of a blind eye, within a few days heard a voice whispering in his ear, saying, "Well, you didn't deserve that, did you?" He thought it was the voice of the Lord, made agreement with it, and began to dwell on his unworthiness. Within hours, his sight in his restored eye was gone.

I like to tell people that grace is undeserved favor; I have heard it said that grace is getting what we don't deserve. I think that's rather negative. I prefer to say that Jesus took what we deserve, so we can have what He deserved.[2]

I encourage you that if you hear that voice, it's the voice of the thief, who is trying to take from you what you just received. I have an entire CD and DVD on this subject called, "The authority to stay free from sickness." It's a full two hours of teaching.

There are so many sick people in the world. How do you know whom and if God wants to heal?

That is a very easy question to answer. If they are sick, then God wants them to experience His healing touch. I don't need a word of knowledge to know that God wants to heal someone. That choice was made over 2,000 years ago. The word of knowledge is a wonderful tool, but it's not the determining factor as to whether God wants to heal someone or not.

Are all Christians called to heal the sick?

Is Jesus the healer? Are we as Christians the dwelling place of God? Then my answer would be yes, for sure. Yet out of our inexperience and not seeing fruit, we have come to the conclusion that God does not want to use us.

A pastor's daughter came to me one night after a meeting and said, "God does not want to use me in healings." I asked how she came to that conclusion. She answered, "As I have prayed for the sick before and not seen them healed."

I replied, "Well, tomorrow night, you are going to be my personal ministry team, and everyone who comes to me for prayer, you are going to heal them." She went extremely pale and tried to come up with excuses for not doing this. She finally agreed and showed up at the meeting.

The first person came to me for prayer after the meeting, and I said, "There you go. Get her healed."

She looked at me like I was an alien. She said, "I don't know what I am doing."

I said, "Neither do I. Asking the lady her name and what is wrong would be a good start." This particular lady had a confirmed leg that was shorter than the other by at least an inch, and it caused her to limp. I said, "Get her to sit down and take a look."

The pastor's daughter looked at me in horror. "What do I do now?" she begged.

I said, "Telling it to grow would be a good start."

She looked at the leg and said, "Grow." It shot out so fast to match the other leg.

The pastor's daughter fell on the floor sobbing and crying because she got the revelation that she has been believing a lie and received the truth that God wanted to use her. I let her cry on the floor for a minute and then said, "OK. That is enough. There's an entire line waiting for me. You heal each of them the same way, and let me know when you are done. I will be up on the front lying down, so it looks like I'm praying, so people won't disturb me because tonight this entire line is yours."

Over an hour later, this young lady came to me so happy, saying, "Guess what? Tonight every person I prayed for got healed." She was simply ecstatic.

Yes, God wants to use every Christian to heal the sick. It's more about our willingness to be used and then stepping outside our comfort zone and letting God be God through us through childlike faith.

How do I finish a prayer off with somebody?

I tell people to pray until they get healed, or you can tell they are not receiving, or you have found yourself now praying from lack. I always want to make sure that I leave the person I am praying for in an encouraging place, never a place of condemnation for not being healed, but always in a place that the door is open to come and receive more ministry.

How do I go about starting a healing ministry in my church?

Each year I run a healing school in Redding for pastors and leaders. I tell them the same thing: "You can learn from the school or from even this book, but you can't go back and tell your senior pastor that what he's doing is all wrong and things need to change."

A couple came to me several years ago and said, "Our pastor does not want us praying for the sick in church, and we believe we are called to this church."

I replied, "Then you best go back and serve his vision." The pastor knew that they were at Bethel and was somewhat concerned about what they might come back and want to do. They then returned to their church and served the senior pastor's vision faithfully.

Within a short period of time, the pastor was so impressed with their hearts that he said, "Why don't you start a small home group for those who are interested in healing?" This was set up, and soon the pastor suggested to them that they take that small group and pray for people after the service on the side of the church. The pastor then e-mailed me and wrote, "I don't know what you told them when they came to Bethel, but whatever it was, I want to say thank you. They came back from Bethel with a heart to serve my vision. Today they help oversee a healing ministry in a fairly large church."

"If you are not in a position to open a Healing Room," I tell people, "then you are a portable Healing Room, for Christ lives in you. Go and heal people outside of the church, and the people around you will see your fruit."

If you are interested in opening a Healing Room, the International Association of Healing Rooms (IAHR) in Spokane, Washington has many resources to help you in your journey.

CONCLUSION

There are many more subjects that I could write on in this book. This was never meant as a comprehensive book on all the ins and outs of the healing ministry. There is still mystery in the healing ministry, and we have to be OK to live in the tension of mystery. What I really wanted to address was the heart of healing and not produce a list of principles. The Kingdom operates by rest, and the more we rest in what Jesus has paid for, the more I am compelled to go after all that Jesus has paid for. When we truly get the revelation of just how much we are loved and how much He loves the world, then something arises in us to give Him away.

Jesus paid much too high aprice for us to just come together, do church, then sit back and do nothing. I want to keep burning bright for Jesus. I want to see the saints arise and come into a revelation of who we are in Him and who He is in us. I long to see the Church awaken to the present reality of the power of the Holy Spirit, so that together we will see cities, your nation, and nations of the world transformed.

Let's set our heart right; let's get lost and overwhelmed in the goodness of God. Let's see the nations come to Jesus because we are so smitten with Him that the supernatural becomes the byproduct of knowing the King.

The message of the Kingdom is going forward, and we are seeing nations impacted.

I would love to hear about your exploits and testimonies. Please visit me on my Facebook at Chris Gore or visit me on www.kingdomreleasers.org

and let me know about your audacious adventures and breakthroughs in walking in the supernatural healing power of Jesus.

NOTES

1. "Jesus healed everyone who came to Him. To accept any other standard is to *bring the Bible down to our level of experience,* and deny the nature of the One who changes not." Bill Johnson, *When Heaven Invades Earth* (Shippensburg, PA: Treasure House, 2003), 115.

2. "Jesus got what I deserved so that I could get what He deserved." Bill Johnson, *The Supernatural Power of a Transformed Mind* (Shippensburg, PA: Destiny Image Publishers, 2005), 105.

CHAPTER 16

CORE VALUES OF A HEALING REVIVALIST

I am the Director of Healing Ministries for Bethel Church, and at the time of writing this book, I have over 900 Healing Rooms workers who minister in teams to an average of 270 people each Saturday morning, 50 people via Skype into the Healing Rooms, and over 400 church prayer ministry team members. In addition to this, I oversee our Pastor on Call team, who pray for people who call in from all over the world. I also oversee a team called Healing Ministry Outreach that goes out to pray for people who are too sick to come to the Healing Rooms or to church. I also oversee our Life Resurrection Team, as not everyone dies in God's timing, so we have a specialized team that believes for the resurrection of the dead. For me it is a joy to do healing conferences all over the world and also run Bethel's healing schools that we conduct in Redding once per year and also take around the world.

Several years ago, I felt that I was to write down a list of the core values in my life. I have mentioned them several times when I have taught and have always received e-mails from people, asking what they are and if they could have a copy. Core values are so important to me. I want to see integrity in the lives of believers and also in the healing ministry. There is no need to embellish the facts of what happened. These core values help me to stay true to who God called me to be. They are not an extensive list, and I am sure that you can add to these, and I also add to them. These are not all about healing, but they are all about the Kingdom. I have written a brief summary on each point. I encourage you to develop a list of your own.

I am always a son (see Matt. 6:9).

Don't do anything for identity. I do things because of identity. Much of the Church does not know that they are sons and daughters, let alone beloved sons and daughters. We are a royal priesthood (see 1 Pet. 2:9).

Fruitfulness flows out of intimacy with the Father.

Principles will always bring a measure of fruit, but intimacy and presence will bring forward a great harvest (see John 15:4).

I don't need to strive for fruit.

Ever seen an apple tree trying to bring forth fruit? Fruitfulness comes from knowing who I am and knowing that I am loved I am loved—He loves and likes me (see 1 John 4:19). It's He in me and me in Him.

On earth as it is in Heaven.

Is it in Heaven? If it's not in Heaven, I don't need to tolerate it here, as it is not from God. Sickness is never from God! (See Matthew 6:10.)

Miracles

Miracles are the gospel. I am selling the gospel short if I see the need for miracles as optional (see Rom. 15:9).

God's sovereignty

My lack of power or results will not be blamed on God's sovereignty. The lack is not on God's side.

Power and integrity

I pray that the power I walk in will not surpass the integrity and character that I have. Character and integrity are so important to me, but walking in a life of power to balance that is just as important.

A life of powerlessness is unnecessary.

My experience must line up with the Bible and the standard of Jesus. Anything else is unbiblical. I will not lower my standard based on my lack of experience.[1]

I am 100 percent successful with every person I minister to.

Success to me is doing something with what God has given me. Whether I see the fruit or not, if I loved, then I was successful.

God is in a good mood.

The church worldwide has taken the image of a God who is angry with the world. God so loved the world (see John 3:16). In our efforts to evangelize the world, we have told the world that if they don't get their lives right with God, they will burn in hell. We then wonder why they are scared to come to church to meet with a God who is angry with them. Do I believe in a hell? Yes, for sure, but God's goodness brings people to repentance (see Rom. 2:4).

He is better than we think, and we need to change the way that we think.[2] Build a culture based on God's goodness. "Taste and see that the Lord is good" (Ps. 34:8).

When I make the *declaration* of His goodness, He always shows up. He told me in 2008 that if I declare His goodness, He will always show off His goodness through me.

I will always be anchored to His goodness. My circumstances will not determine His goodness.

Build a culture that lives on the testimony.

Live on the testimony and feast on His goodness. Understand the power of the testimony (see Rev. 19:10; Ps. 119:111). It's impossible to pray and have nothing happen if I love.

Always stay childlike.

I want to remain a novice. If I become good at my job or professional, then there is no need for God's empowering grace.

WALKING IN SUPERNATURAL HEALING POWER

Sowing and reaping

It's never my glory when the sick are healed, and it's never my burden and responsibility when they are not. When I sow, the plough is always attracted to the seed.

Open Heaven

Where I go, He comes and when He comes, He does good things because He's a good God in a good mood (see Isa. 64; Mark 1). "Christ in you, the hope of glory" (Col. 1:27).

No crying out for an open Heaven like there is something else He needs to do. Yes, I will pray for rain in the day of latter rain.

Be revival.

Rather than crying out to God for revival like He needs to do something else, I am a walking revival. Don't wait for revival; be revival (see Acts 12). Peter's family is crying out for his release from prison, yet Peter is already out! When Peter knocks on the door after getting out of prison, they say, "You are beside yourself. It can't be Peter as we are praying for Peter's release." Are you praying for revival because you don't know that you already are a walking revival? Revival is knocking at the door. Let's just burn and have revival.

Revival is family.

What good is it if I win the world and lose my family?

A culture of honor

See people how God sees them, and treat them like God would treat them. It starts at the top and comes down. I treat every person how God sees them and how I would want to be treated. Honor the gifts and calling on their lives.

When I learn to honor people, I position myself to become the floor to other people's ceilings.

A culture of joy

Righteousness, peace, and joy. Joy is an inside job. I don't need external circumstances to determine if I will be joyful.

I am never the judge.

It's never my place to judge; my role is to love.

A culture of empowerment to every person

Every person in the church is empowered to do the works of Jesus. *Every person is significant!*

Understanding of the Father's heart

It's always God's will to heal. He never allows sickness or creates sickness. He can only give what He has. Sickness is not to develop character. (See Hebrews 1:3.)

If we think that it's not always God's will to heal, then how can we really come with expectation in our hearts when ministering to the sick that He will heal?

To the leper, He says, "I am willing," and His words still resound today (see Matt. 8:3).

A culture of thanksgiving

Thanksgiving always increases the Kingdom (see Matt. 15:36).

A culture of grace

The law was fulfilled, and now there is a revival of grace and mercy. Don't wait for the conditions to be perfect or the people to be perfect. (See John 19:30.)

I am totally dependent on His grace.

"It's no longer I who live, but Christ lives in me" (Gal. 2:20). That's grace. Without Christ, I can do nothing.

A culture of freedom

With a culture of freedom, I won't put myself in a position to control what is revival and what is not. When I put myself in this position, I am making myself an expert on revival and then the one most liable to miss it.

With a culture of freedom, there are always messes made. We tell our people they can make as big a mess as they are prepared to tidy up.

God's timing

Today is the day of salvation and healing. God's timing was 2,000 years ago when Jesus hung on the cross and cried out, "It is finished."

Faith is not the only reason He heals.

While faith is the currency of Heaven, it's not the only reason He heals. He heals because He loves us.

Every person I meet and pray for will have an encounter with love.

Gospel is power and love, not love without power and not power without love.

Never leave anyone in condemnation over why they were not healed.

It's not just my faith or their faith. Always encourage and never leave in the bondage of "just believe."

The key to more

"Give, and it will be given" (Luke 6:38). If you want the more, give away everything that you have. It's my mandate to give away and train, empower, touch, and love as many people as I can.

Live my dreams.

I believe in living my dreams and helping others to fulfill theirs.

Prophetic voice

When I prophesy, my role is to always bring out the gold in people. I will never bring out the dirt. People already know their dirt. Why do they need me to reinforce it? It does not take much prophetic discernment to prophesy dirt, but it takes someone looking from God's perspective to see the gold.

Generosity

I will sacrifice my own standard of living before I will withdraw from being generous. I will always live generously.

Inheritance

I am building an inheritance for a generation I may never see. Revelation between generations will not be lost.

NOTES

1. "Jesus healed everyone who came to Him. To accept any other standard is to *bring the Bible down to our level of experience,* and deny the nature of the One who changes not." Bill Johnson, *When Heaven Invades Earth* (Shippensburg, PA: Treasure House, 2003), 115.
2. "He's better than we think, so let's change the way we think." Bill Johnson, *Face to Face with God* (Lake Mary, FL: Charisma House, 2007), 195.

ABOUT CHRIS GORE

Chris was a pastor in New Zealand before coming to Bethel where he graduated from Bethel School of Supernatural Ministry. He is currently the Director of Healing Ministries. While having an unquenchable hunger for His presence, Chris' passion is to see the church walk in a kingdom mindset and see ordinary saints equipped to walk in extraordinary exploits by releasing the kingdom through healings and miracles. His heart is to see churches, cities, and nations transformed. He is married to an amazing wife, Liz, and has three wonderful daughters, Charlotte, Emma, and Sophie.

www.kingdomreleasers.org

Facebook: www.facebook.com/ChrissGore

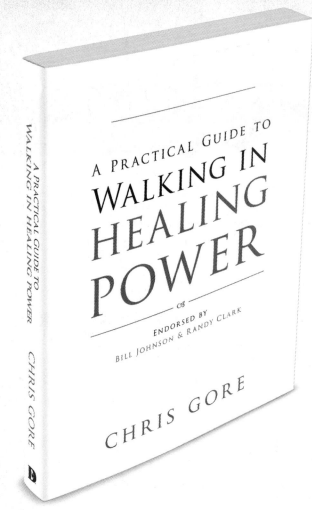

A PRACTICAL GUIDE TO
WALKING IN
HEALING
POWER

ENDORSED BY
BILL JOHNSON & RANDY CLARK

CHRIS GORE

GO DEEPER

Want to learn more?
Get the in-depth manual and discover how you
can walk in supernatural healing power today!